MW00709493

Robert Irwin's Pocket Guide for Home Buyers

Other McGraw-Hill Books by Robert Irwin

Robert Irwin's Pocket Guide for Home Buyers

101 Questions and Answers for Every Home Buyer

Robert Irwin

McGraw-Hill

New York   San Francisco   Washington, D.C.   Auckland   Bogotá
Caracas   Lisbon   London   Madrid   Mexico City   Milan
Montreal   New Delhi   San Juan   Singapore
Sydney   Tokyo   Toronto

Library of Congress Cataloging-in-Publication Data
Irwin, Robert.
    [Pocket guide for home buyers]
    Robert Irwin's pocket guide for home buyers :
    101 questions and answers
    for every home buyer / Robert Irwin.
        p   cm.
    ISBN 0-07-032945-1 (alk. paper)
    1. House buying—United States. I. Title.
HD1379.I658 1998
643'.12—dc21   97-49299
                                                  CIP

Mcgraw-Hill

A Division of The McGraw·Hill Companies

1 2 3 4 5 6 7 8 9 0   FGR/FGR   9 0 3 2 1 0 9 8

ISBN 0-07-032945-1

*The sponsoring editor for this book was Susan Barry, the edit-
ing supervisor was Patricia V. Amoroso, and the production
supervisor was Clare B. Stanley. It was set in Palatino by
Donald Feldman of McGraw-Hill's Professional Book Group
composition unit.*

Printed and bound by Quebecor/Fairfield.

 This book is printed on recycled, acid-free paper
containing a minimum of 50% recycled, de-inked
fiber.

Contents

Preface

Buying a home can be aggravating, confusing, intimidating, and financially dangerous—in short, it can be a harrowing experience... unless you know what you're doing.

Understanding the home buying process well enough to control it, however, is difficult. That's especially the case if this is your first home purchase, or if it's been a few years since you last bought a home. The rules of the game have changed; they've gotten trickier and more complex. Now you need to understand legally complicated purchase documents, handle inspections and savvy sellers, deal with sophisticated agents, and a whole lot more. In fact, with the increase in housing prices, buying a home now is not only one of the most important financial transactions you'll make in your lifetime, it also can be one of the most strenuous.

Of course, there's a lot of advice out there. There are books and gurus aplenty to tell you what you ought to do. However, I've found that most of what they say is complicated and difficult to understand.

Furthermore, buyers with whom I've talked have expressed frustration with the long and complicated answers that are frequently given to their simple questions. "What's needed," I've heard more than once, "is a concise explanation—a simple answer in just a few words, something I can take along with me when I look at houses and when I talk to sellers and deal with agents."

That's the idea behind this book. I've listed what I've found to be the 101 most often asked home buying questions. Then I've given my opinion in two forms: first, a short, concise paragraph, a quick answer. Then, for those who want the details, an expanded answer considering many of the consequences and options involved.

This is not a hard book. It's not even a heavy book. You can take it with you on your home search and consult it wherever you are. Remember, you don't need the answer to your question later on, tomorrow, or next week. You need the answer now.

If you're house hunting, don't feel you're alone with no one truly on your side. This book will give you confidence, information, and insight into how to successfully, and profitably, buy a home. It will alert you to dangers in the deal and point out opportunities for gain. It will guide you toward getting the home you want for the price you want to pay.

Robert Irwin's Pocket Guide for Home Buyers

1

How Do I Pick a Great Agent?

1. How Do I Check Out the Agent I've Selected?

The Quick Answer

Ask the agent several questions such as, "How long have you been in the business?" It usually takes three to five years to get up to speed in real estate sales. The longer in the business, chances are the more successful the agent has been. "Are you active or part-time?" You want a full-time agent working for you. "How many properties did you sell in the last 12 months?" One a month, on average, is a good indicator. If fewer, ask why? If the agent begins complaining about the market, the lack of integrity of buyers, how tough the field is—maybe you should look elsewhere. You want someone who is successful already, not someone struggling to survive.

The Expanded Answer

In real estate, as in most other selling fields, 20 percent of the people do 80 percent of the business. You want one of those 20 percent agents.

In addition in real estate, more so than in most other fields, there are many part-timers. These are often people who have retired on pensions from other fields and are looking to pick up a few extra dollars. They may be fine folks, but I doubt many have their whole heart in the business. It's too easy for them to simply walk away from the tough deals (or the tough moments in a deal). It's also often too much effort to do the necessary leg work to keep up on the market.

When an agent tells you that he or she has sold a lot of properties (an agent with whom I was dealing the other day honestly told me she had sold more than 50 properties in the preceding year—that's about one a week!), check it out. Ask to see the sales records. That's not an unreasonable request.

Then ask for the names and phone numbers of half a dozen of the agent's recent clients. No agent should balk at giving you these—the agent should be proud to offer them.

Now, call several. Just say the agent gave you their name as a recommendation. How did they like working with the agent? Was the arrangement successful? Profitable?

No, the agent isn't likely to give you the name of someone with whom they had a problem. But, just being able to provide half a dozen names of clients in the past six months is in itself a kind of recommendation.

Also, check to be sure that your agent is computer literate. Today most real estate boards are completely computerized. Your agent should be able to almost instantaneously give you printouts of listings of all the houses in your price range and area and with the features you require. It's not like the old days when you had to plow through thick listing books or search through streets endlessly. Today your agent should be able to narrow your search quickly and effectively in just a few minutes before a computer screen. Ask your agent about this. If he or she doesn't or can't do it, you may want to look elsewhere.

Finally, check your own reactions. You are going to want an agent assertive enough to get you a good deal. But not so aggressive that he or she intimidates you into accepting something you'd rather not have. It's a fine line, and it's different for each person. Basically, you're *not* looking for a friend or confident. You want an informed adviser and advocate.

2. Where Do I Find a Good Agent?

The Quick Answer

Look in the same place you would to find a good attorney, stock broker, insurance agent, or other professional. In other words, try to get recommendations from people you trust (relatives, friends, other professionals, even a new employer). Use the phone book yellow pages or newspaper advertising only as a last resort.

The Expanded Answer

As in a barrel of apples, there are good and bad agents in real estate. The vast majority are good, but if you run into a bad apple, it can cost you a great deal.

Personal recommendations should be your first choice. If you liked a real estate agent with whom you worked in the past and are moving to a different area, often that first agent will be able to recommend a good agent to work with in your new area. (The old agent will be eager to help, since he or she could get a piece of the commission when you buy, particularly if you are dealing with a national chain!) The old agent will probably recommend a broker agent who has taken advanced training, such as the courses offered by the National Association of Realtors®.

If you have relatives or friends in the new area, most will have had some dealings with agents and can steer you to those they liked. Usually these recommendations are straightforward, but not necessarily. Years ago, some agents used to tell their former clients that they would give them something like a hundred silver dollars for a recommendation. Today, however, with commissions running into the tens of thousands of dollars, most people won't be looking to make a hundred bucks to recommend someone they consider less than reputable.

Finally, you may already have a professional relationship with someone in the new area—an attorney, insurance agent, accountant, employer. My experience is that generally speaking, good people tend to hang out together. If there's a professional whom I like and trust, I tend to rely on that person's recommendation.

If all else fails, you can attempt the old method of picking a large, active-looking office that has lots of agents. Walk in and ask to speak to the broker. This is important because in almost all offices, agents, particularly those who are less successful, will pull "counter time" or "up time." This means they must stay in the office and wait for potential clients who walk in over the transom. If you take the current "up" or "counter" agent, it's the luck of the draw.

But, if you ask to speak to the broker, you'll be sent to the person who actually runs the office (or helps run it in a big office). Then, simply ask for the name of their number one agent, the one who has sold (not listed) more property in the last year than any other.

The broker may chuckle at your brashness, but it's a straightforward question and chances are you'll be given a straight answer. When you have the name, call that person. (Chances are that agent is out in the field and not sitting around the office.)

3. Should I Work with a Buyer's Agent?

The Quick Answer

If possible, it's a good idea. A buyer's agent has you for the client. A seller's agent has the seller for the client. One of the oldest maxims is that no one can truly serve two masters. When it comes to critical negotiations or judgment calls, who would you rather have the agent working for—you or the seller?

The Expanded Answer

In the old days, agents almost always worked for the sellers. That is, they had a fiduciary or trust relationship with the sellers. What this meant was that if you offered $90,000 for a house, but in confidence told the agent you'd really be willing to pay $100,000, the agent was ethically and legally bound to inform the seller of what you'd said. Now, what do you think your chances would be of getting that property for $90,000?!

Your only choice was to keep your mouth shut. Today, you can find a buyer's agent. A buyer's agent has a fiduciary or trust relationship to you. The agent ethically and legally should not tell the seller that you'd pay more. On the other hand, if the seller admits to this agent that they'd really be willing to accept $85,000, the agent must tell you! That's a huge advantage.

There's also a middle road today allowed in some states in which the agent can, theoretically, serve both buyer and seller—a "dual agent." This is murky territory and in attempting to avoid hurting either party by not passing along vital information, he or she could conceivably end up harming both. In a dual-agency arrangement, the agent attempts to protect both the buyers and the sellers.

The agent must declare whom he or she is serving. In many states this takes the form of a written document given to all parties. It's important to remember that who pays the agent doesn't determine whom the agent serves. Just because the seller is paying the commission, doesn't mean that the agent isn't working for you. It's whom the agent declares himself or herself for that counts.

What this means is that very often you can use a buyer's agent, yet don't have to pay that agent anything. Rather, the buyer's agent works for you and then, assuming the property is listed, gets a part of the listing commission from the seller. [On the other hand, you might have to pay. For example, if you buy a property for sale by owner (FSBO) and the sellers refuse to pay any commission, you might have to pay your buyer's agent.]

Finally, one of the not so obvious advantages of a buyer's agent is that this person often will be better able to find just the right house for you, including FSBOs.

On the other hand, some buyer's agents aren't worth the agreement they have you sign. Recently a friend was selling a home FSBO and was presented an offer $7000 below asking price. My friend was willing to pay the buyer's agent a half-listing fee, in this case $2\frac{1}{2}$ percent. But, the buyer's agent wanted a full 5 percent. So the agent said that since she knew the buyers would pay full price, my friend (the seller) should counter with a full-price offer, then pay her (the agent) the additional $7000 as a commission. Remember, she was presumably representing the buyers in all this, but was in reality screwing them out of $7000 in order to fatten her commission!

Certainly this example is an exception, but it's worth remembering that just because an agent says on a piece of paper that she or he is in a position of trust to you, doesn't mean it's guaranteed in real life. (By the way, if an agent works for you as a buyer's agent, you're the client. The seller is the customer.)

4. How Much Should I Pay a Buyer's Agent?

The Quick Answer

It is completely negotiable. It is absolutely true in every locale in the United States and in dealing with every agent that there is *no set fee*. Agents and real estate companies cannot get together and set a fee that they all will charge. Having said that, however, keep in mind that agents can say how much is the minimum they will work for and refuse to work for you unless you are willing to pay their minimum amount.

The Expanded Answer

While there is no official set fee, there is usually a "going rate" that most agents charge. This is not to imply that there is any collusion between agents. It's simply a matter of the marketplace and competition at work. When sellers list their houses, that fee generally runs between 5 and 7 percent of the selling price for a full-service broker. If the seller is willing to do some of the sales work, such as pay for advertising and show the property, that fee can drop down, usually to between 3 and 4 percent.

When you hire a buyer's broker you may need to pay that person a fee. While it's true that the buyer's broker may be able to ultimately get his or her fee out the seller's pocket, it may not always be the case. As noted in a previous example, your buyer's agent may find you the perfect house that's FSBO, and the owner may refuse to pay any commission. In that case you may be stuck paying the agent's fee, even though you're the buyer! The amount is usually half the going fee in the area, often between 2½ and 3 percent.

Many buyer's agents will ask you to sign an agreement designating them as your exclusive right-to-buy agent. The agreement may specify that for a set period of time (it should always have a time period), you will pay a commission to the agent regardless of whether the agent finds you a house or you find one yourself. (No fee is usually paid if you don't buy.) This is to protect the agent from finding an unlisted house for you and then having you go around the agent's back and buy directly from a FSBO seller.

Some agents want an up-front amount of money, say $1000, to get started looking, the amount to be refunded from the commission if you eventually buy. I would never pay an agent an up-front fee. If the agent doesn't have the wherewithal to front his or her own money to operate the business, I surely don't want to be in the position of doing so.

Furthermore, unless it was a particularly difficult market or I was looking for a very specific, difficult-to-find piece of property, I'd think twice about signing a long-term buyer's agency agreement in which I agreed to pay a commission to a buyer's agent no matter what, even if I found the home. Today there are too many good agents out there looking for business for me as a buyer to tie myself up in such a way to just one.

5. Should I Go to an Independent or a Franchise Broker?

The Quick Answer

The general rule is that it's the agent, not the office that's most important. Go with the best agent you can find, independent or franchise. However, if you don't know any agents and can't get a recommendation, the national franchises usually maintain at least minimal quality control, have procedures that protect both them and you, and usually have heavy errors-and-omission insurance in case one of their agents makes a bad mistake.

The Expanded Answer

Today it's very hard for an independent office to survive. National franchises such as Coldwell Banker, Century 21, R/EMax and others offer heavy advertising, name-brand recognition, and legal support and associated services to agents. They often overwhelm small independent offices with their competition.

As a result, most agents today in most areas belong to a franchise of one sort or another. My own experience has been that only those independents that are either extremely strong, with excellent agents, or very weak, with poor agents, have not been gobbled up by one or the other of the franchises. That usually means that if you're dealing with an independent, you've probably got the best, or the worst, of the field.

It's important to understand, however, that although you may go with a national name in real estate, in most states you're still dealing with a local office. For example, a broker friend of mine had successfully operated an independent office near Los Angeles for over 20 years. He had seven agents working full-time for him, every one a winner.

However, he decided that he could make more money with less effort by associating with a national franchise. So one day, he simply converted. His office now bears both the national name and his own name. It's a franchise, he's still the broker in charge and the agents are the same. He operates under the umbrella of the national firm, which provides the support noted above, but you still deal with him or one of his associated agents. In a sense, you're getting the best of both worlds.

Except...the national franchise has strict rules regarding the amount of commission charged, how deals are handled, where escrows are placed, and so forth. My friend no longer has the flexibility he once had to tailor-make a deal to suit his clients and customers. Today, he follows the rules. This sometimes benefits those clients and customers, and other times it causes them grief and produces a poorer result.

6. What Do the Terms *Agent*, *Broker*, and *Realtor* Mean, and How Do Commission Splits Work?

The Quick Answer

Anyone who offers to sell, or rent real estate for another person (for money) in any state must be licensed. The generic term for such a person is an *agent*. One who can open an office and operate independently as an agent is a *broker*. A person who must work under a broker's tutelage is a salesperson. A broker who also belongs to the National Association of Realtors, a trade organization, is called a Realtor®. This designation is a registered trademark and can be used only by members of the association.

The Expanded Answer

In order to become a broker in most states, a person must not only pass a rigorous exam (sometimes lasting several days), but must also be able to show several years experience in the field as a salesperson working under another broker. (In some states a college degree or similar achievement will satisfy the experience requirement—not a good thing in this author's opinion.) In order to become a salesperson, one must also pass a usually rigorous exam. In addition, in most states in order to renew their licenses every four years or so, all agents must take course work to keep up on the latest developments in areas such as contracts, agency, fair housing, handling money held in trust, ethics, and consumer affairs.

In spite of the best efforts of states to regulate the industry, however, a few bad apples always get through. The bulletins published by state real estate agencies regularly list hundreds of agents who have been disciplined for making errors that have hurt their clients.

It is important to understand that agents regularly split the commissions they get. As a result, that huge commission that (usually) sellers pay ends up not being quite so huge for the individual agent.

For example, let's say a home sells for $200,000, and the commission is 6 percent or $12,000. That seems like a hefty sum. But if there are two offices involved, one that had the listing and another that found the buyer, the commission is usually split down the center, each office getting half, or $6000.

And assuming that the broker wasn't involved directly, but that the office was represented by a salesperson, the commission is split in half again—half to the office, half to the salesperson, or $3000 apiece. In addition, there may be franchise fees and other costs deducted.

As a result, the agent with whom you deal may end up getting only 1½ percent of the sales price when there's a 6 percent commission. In our example, that comes to $3000 or less. Suddenly those commissions may not seem quite so large. (Of course, other splits may be used as agreed upon between the agents.)

7. How Do I Help an Agent Help Me Find the Right House?

The Quick Answer

Be forthcoming with information about what it is you want. If you really must have four bedrooms, don't waste everyone's time looking at three-bedroom houses. If you want a specific neighborhood, don't go looking around in other neighborhoods. If you want a one-story house, don't spend time looking at split-level or two-story buildings. Tell you agent up front, "I want four bedrooms, in the Healthy Springs area, on a single level."

The Expanded Answer

There's the old saw about a patient who goes into the doctor's office and sits down. The doctor asks, "So, what's wrong with you today?" To which the patient replies, "You're the doctor...you tell me!"

The problem is that often we don't really know what's wrong ourselves; we don't really know what we want. Thus, a part of the house-hunting process is actually discovery. By seeing what's available on the market, we can come to realize what we don't like and, conversely, what we are really searching for.

It is for this reason that good agents will often ask right at the onset, "Is this the first time you've looked, or have you been out house hunting before?" They want to know where in the search process they've contacted you. If it's your first time, a good agent will plan a broad spectrum of homes to look at, to help you narrow down what it is you want. If you've looked before, the agent will expect you to be able to provide a more succinct explanation of what it is you want. Remember, the more correct, detailed information you can give your agent about your desires and needs, the better able he or she will be to satisfy them.

There is also the matter of feedback when walking through homes. Don't be a shy or quiet buyer. When you like something, tell the agent. When you dislike something, say that, too. A good agent is listening carefully and soon puts together a list of your likes and dislikes. This helps that agent prepare the next tour for you, eliminating houses you obviously won't like, adding in those you may go for.

Remember, it's your money. Don't settle for less than you want and can get.

8. Should I Work with Only One Agent or Many?

The Quick Answer

You should find an agent whom you like and trust and work with him or her…until that agent stops working for you. A good agent will remain loyal to you for months, sometimes years. Other agents, however, will drop you if you don't quickly find and buy a home through them.

The Expanded Answer

Ask any agent and chances are the one thing they dislike most about real estate is buyer disloyalty. The stories are legend of agents who put in countless hours and miles searching for just the right home for buyers only to discover that at the last minute, the buyers find another home somewhere else and use a different agent to purchase it. Remember, the agent only gets paid when you buy through him or her. (In some rare cases the agent may be entitled to a portion of a commission if they showed you a listed property first, even though you bought through a different agent.)

On the other hand, what agents often fail to mention or even recognize, is agent disloyalty (not to be confused with violating their fiduciary trust to their clients, discussed elsewhere). I know some perfectly fine agents who make excellent livings in real estate who have a three-strike rule. It works like this: They will meet a buyer the first time and qualify them—determine what they are looking for and how much they can afford. The first strike.

They will then arrange to show that buyer every conceivable property in the buyer's price range and area of interest. Strike two.

If the buyers don't purchase one of those homes the first time out, the agent will then try to determine if the buyer was qualified wrong, if they are truly interested in purchasing, or if there are other properties that the buyer didn't have time or energy to see. If appropriate, they will go out with the buyer one more time to show property. If the buyer on this second trip still doesn't find a house they want to buy, it's three strikes and you're out.

The agent will leave saying something such as, "I know just what you're looking for and as soon as it comes on the market, I'll call you. In the meantime, if you see anything at all you like, give me a call and we'll talk about it." The translation is, don't expect me to call you, but if you really do find something you want to buy, call me so I can collect the commission. That's agent disloyalty.

These agents are looking for the quick deal, the motivated buyer ready to make a move, today. If you're not that person, they move on.

If your agent is not loyal to you, does not make an effort to look daily for properties for you, confer with you weekly (or several times a week), show you property every weekend without your having to call and beg, drop them. After all, chances are they've dropped you.

Remember, a good, loyal agent will be there for you all the time. And you'll recognize this and will want to be sure that this agent gets the commission when you buy.

9. What Is the Difference between Sellers and Listers?

The Quick Answer

There are two sides to playing the real estate business, for agents. On one side are those who make a living, often a good one, by just listing property. They are called *listers*. On the other hand, there are others who make most of their living finding buyers and putting together deals. Those are called *sellers*. As a buyer, you are better off dealing with a seller than a lister.

The Expanded Answer

The old maxim is, "Those who list, last."

The point is that in order to survive in the highly competitive real estate business, an agent needs listings. They are the bread and butter of the business. Even when the market is bad, if an agent has listings, something will sell and bring in enough money to keep the business going. As a result, all agents strive to have listings.

However, some agents have discovered that you can do better than just survive by concentrating on listings alone—you can do quite well. They will often "farm" a very large area, go door-to-door meeting the locals, join civic organizations, advertise in grocery stores to get their name known, and so on. What they are after are listings, lots of them. Too often when they get one, however, they will simply put it on the *multiple* (where agents list properties on which they will "cobroke," or cooperate with other agents). Listers hope, and anticipate, that someone else will sell their properties while they're off to find another listing.

This type of agent will, of course, work with a buyer such as you, if you suddenly pop up and seem eager and anxious. But, too often this agent has inadequate skills in locating just the property you want and negotiating the best price and terms for you.

Ideally you want a seller, an agent who, besides taking listings, has honed his or her skills in working with buyers and getting them the best deal possible.

How do you tell the two apart? Ask the agent how many listings they took (not just those that sold) in the last 12 months. Then ask how many properties they sold which they did not have listed? You should get your answer immediately.

10. How Much Should I Tell My Agent about My Finances?

The Quick Answer

You need to tell your agent enough to allow him or her to qualify you as to price and terms. Most of us believe we know how much we want to pay. But, unless you're in the business or quite sophisticated in terms of real estate finance, you may not actually know how much you can afford. It could turn out to be more, or less, than you think. You need to tell your agent enough so that he or she can come up with a price and the type of financing to suit you.

The Expanded Answer

Our finances are very personal. Most of us feel uncomfortable sharing them with anyone. We don't even like sharing them with our banker (but know that's often a necessity). And though we may be dealing with an agent whom we like and trust to find us a property, we may still not feel comfortable revealing the delicate intricacies of our money matters. That could be a problem.

How much can you afford to pay for a house? The answer is a combination of how much you can put down and how big a mortgage you can get. Do you know the correct answers? If not, then your agent can help you find them.

As an alternative, if you're a prime buyer (no bad credit, good job, money in the bank), you can simply go to a mortgage broker and get a letter stating how big a loan you can get. This will tell an agent how much mortgage you can get and with the knowledge that you have 20 percent or 10 percent to put down, they can easily qualify you for a home. (The lender's letter is also very helpful when negotiating with a seller! See also *Chapter 4* on financing.)

On the other hand, if your credit isn't wonderful, you don't have much for a down payment, and/or your job prospects are less than certain, it could be a different story. Now you may need "creative financing" or help from the seller to buy. Usually it takes an agent to arrange this. However, the agent must know your financial situation in order to do it.

In short, in many cases you'll need to explain your financial circumstances, perhaps in great detail, to your agent so that he or she will know how to help you. In my experience, I have found it extremely rare that clients who tell a licensed agent about their personal finance end up having a complaint. Remember, the only reason the agent wants to know how much money you have to put down, how big a monthly payment you can handle, and what your credit is like is (presumably) in order to "qualify" you, to determine which houses you can actually afford to buy.

On the other hand, many agents are hesitant to come right out and ask for personal financial information. Most won't ask a direct question such as, "What's your gross income?" or "What are your monthly expenses?" But nevertheless, they need to know that information, and you may need to tell them, even to volunteer it!

If you don't want to tell an agent about your personal finances, you have to ask yourself this question: If I trust an agent to negotiate what will probably be the biggest purchase of my lifetime, my house, why shouldn't I trust that agent with my personal financial information?

11. Do I Want My Agent to Be Pushy or Meek and Mild Mannered?

The Quick Answer

Your agent has two main functions: the first is to find you the home of your dreams (or at least something close); the second is to negotiate the best deal for you. You want an agent who is compatible enough with your personality, who works easily with you, so that he or she will know what you want and find it. At the same time, you want an agent who, once you've found the right home, is aggressive enough to go out there and get the seller to accept an offer favorable to you.

The Expanded Answer

One of the biggest complaints that I hear about agents is that they can sometimes be overly assertive. I've talked with buyers who have said that some of the agents they've dealt with seemed to have their own agenda. If the buyers rejected property after property, the agent would become increasingly irritated. The agent would suggest that the buyers ought to make up their minds more quickly or, since they've seen all the properties the agent has to show, they should pick one, now. Otherwise, by implication (if not downright statement), they were wasting the agent's time.

You don't have to put up with that, and you shouldn't. A good agent won't attempt to push you into something you don't want. A good agent will simply present properties to you.

You can easily tell when an agent is compatible with you. Going out and looking at houses, if not outright fun, will at least be a rewarding experience. You won't feel threatened, intimidated, or pushed into anything. Yes, the agent may indicate that the home is a good price for the market or that a particular home is well situated or otherwise tell you which home they think is a better buy, but the good agent will give you room and time to make your own decision. If you don't feel completely comfortable going out with an agent, drop that person like a hot potato.

On the other hand, the danger is that an agent who is obsequious, too submissive, or too easygoing and friendly will not be a strong enough advocate for you when it comes time to present your offer to the seller. If they're weak with you, how will they be with a seller (and seller's agent) who may demand a too high price and strict terms?

Ideally you want an agent who is firm, but not harsh. (Every now and then you want to see the glint of steel in the agent's eyes!) If you're misinterpreting the market (thinking that houses are worth less than they really are), a good agent will firmly straighten you out. If you think a house is wonderful, but it has a drainage problem, the agent will forcefully make you see the downside of buying it. In other words, a good agent will be friendly, but strong; patient, but assertive in making things clear; open to your desires and wishes, but forceful when it comes to preventing you from making a mistake.

That's the kind of agent who will represent you well both when looking for a house and when you make your offer.

12. When Is It Time to Switch Agents?

The Quick Answer

You should switch when you feel an agent either isn't working hard for you or doesn't really know what you want. An agent who's working hard for you will let you know it. She or he will show you every house on the market you might be interested in. Such agents will make themselves available when it's convenient for you to tour homes, whether on weekends or evenings. If you can't find anything initially, they will call you at least weekly telling you about any price reductions or new homes on the market. At the same time, you will feel that they know just what you want, sometimes better than you! They won't show you property you would never consider. When an agent falls down on either count, drop that person.

The Expanded Answer

I've known agents who've worked hard with buyers for six months or more, until just the right house was found. I myself have worked with agents in an unfamiliar area who, I thought, did such an exemplary job that I have actually paid them an unsolicited bonus upon close of escrow!

On the other hand, I've talked with buyers who, after the first tour of properties, had the agent essentially blow them off. The agent gave the buyer a card and said something such as, "I'll be looking for houses for you and as soon as something comes along that fits, I'll call you." Then, the buyers hear nothing, sometimes for months. When the agent breaks off weekly (at minimum) contact, you can assume the agent is no longer working hard for you. You should feel free to contact other agents.

On the other hand, it's just as important that an agent understands what you really want. I've talked with buyers who were extremely dissatisfied with agents who apparently worked hard, but showed them the wrong types of properties. The agent simply didn't listen to what the buyers were saying. Often these incompetent agents showed buyers properties they (the agent) liked, instead of what the buyers wanted. When the agent and you don't fit, look elsewhere. (Sometimes an agent who doesn't fit with your needs won't get the idea and may pester you. You may simply have to be open and honest—tell her or him, "I appreciate your efforts, but I don't believe you understand what I want and I'm not going to work with you anymore." Your honesty may actually help the agent with future clients.)

It's also important to remember that agents normally don't get paid a dime unless and until they make a sale. Thus all the time they spend on you (and time really is money to them) is hope and prayer for them. An agent who feels you are a serious buyer is usually willing to put forth the effort, in the hope that you will eventually buy from them.

On the other hand, it's a two-way street. If the agent feels you are simply window-shopping and don't really want to buy, or can't buy, you can't expect them to work hard on your behalf. Further, if an agent calls you weekly and you express a lack of interest in buying a house and seem turned off about making an offer on any properties, don't expect them to be too enthused about spending a lot more time on you. Thus how hard an agent works for you (assuming she or he is good at the job) is going to depend in a large part on how good a buyer you really are.

2
How Do I Find Just the Right House?

13. Ask Yourself, "How Long Do I Plan to Live in My Next Home?"

The Quick Answer

Most people plan on living in their next home forever. However, that's usually unrealistic. A job change, more kids, children growing up and leaving home, the desire to move on, illness, financial problems, or other reasons may make your term of ownership shorter than you originally anticipated. If you can foresee moving within the next two to three years, renting may be more financially advantageous than buying.

The Expanded Answer

Except when the market is extremely hot and prices are shooting up, you don't want to be buying and selling homes very often. The reason is the transaction costs. Buying a home, including the finance charges, can cost 4 to 7 percent of the purchase price. Selling a home including an agent's commission can cost 8 to 10 percent. The reality is that it can cost 12 to 17 percent of a home's value to buy and resell it. The question becomes, how long must you live in the house to recoup your transaction costs?

The answer has everything to do with the rate of appreciation. During the early 1990s, there was negative appreciation—homes went down in value. During those days recent home buyers not only did not break even, many lost significant amounts of money when they resold.

Recently, housing prices have been going up. While the appreciation has been higher than 10 percent in some few areas, that type of increase tends to be a short-lived spike. More reasonable increases in a good market are 3 to 5 percent annually. If we assume a healthy 4 percent a year, that means that it will take three to five years to just break even when you sell, after paying closing costs.

Another way of saying this is that financially speaking, if you're looking short term, it's probably cheaper to rent than to buy. This is particularly true when you add in the potential interest you could receive by sticking the down payment and closing costs money in the bank instead of in the house.

Of course, home owners have the advantage over renters in that they can deduct property taxes and mortgage interest (up to very high maximums) from their personal income taxes. However, that is usually more than offset by the fact that, generally speaking, renting is almost always cheaper than buying. Often you can rent a house for about two-thirds of what it costs the owner, monthly, to own it. For example, if you're renting a house for $1200 a month, chances are it's costing the owner about $1800 to keep it (including loan payment, taxes, insurance, repairs, and utilities). These costs usually amount to more than the income tax deduction for property taxes and mortgage interest that the owners get.

This is not to say that home ownership isn't wonderful. There's also the issues of privacy and security that owning affords. Many people feel that those intangibles are worth every penny. It must be said, however, that if you're looking at it short term, ownership may not be as good a financial deal as it has been cracked up to be.

14. Ask Yourself, "What Do I Want in a House?"

The Quick Answer

Make a wish list. Put down every feature that you would like to have from a jacuzzi tub in the master bath to a three-car garage. From close to shopping to good schools. Then prioritize your wish list. If you have 15 or 20 items on the list, rank them from 1 (the most desired) to 15 (the least desired). Finally, take your top three items and make that your "must-have list." See if you can get those items in your next home. If you can, then expand your must-have list to the next three and so on.

The Expanded Answer

It's important to remember that there's always a difference between what we want and what we can get, regardless of our income and assets. None of us can always have everything. Which is to say, we need to determine what's most important to us. We need to prioritize between what we desire and what we absolutely must have. If you can do this before you go looking for a house, you can save yourself a lot of time and some sore feet.

You can use the following list to help you determine your precise wants. (I've filled in a few suggestions to get you started—feel free to cross them out and replace them with others, if you choose.)

Wants List

Priority

1. Good schools _____
2. Close to work _____
3. Safe neighborhood _____
4. Three or four bedrooms _____
5. Two or more baths _____
6. Large/small back yard _____
7. Two/three car garage _____
8. Low dues (for condo) _____
9. Big kitchen _____
10. Easy flowing design _____
11. _____
12. _____
13. _____
14. _____
15. _____
16. _____
17. _____
18. _____
19. _____
20. _____

15. Which Should I Buy: A Condo, Detached house, Co-op, or Townhouse?

The Quick Answer

The choice is between independent living and shared ownership. Each has advantages and detracting features. In terms of price, often some form of shared ownership, such as a condo, will have a lower price than detached homes in the same neighborhood, allowing you to get in easier. Just remember, however, that what's cheaper when you buy is also going to bring less when you sell.

The Expanded Answer

In a detached house you are lord of your castle. You have maximum privacy. When you live in a building that is shared by others (a condo or co-op for example), you often have common walls so noise from neighbors may sometimes come through. There may be shared driveways, and certainly if there are facilities such as tennis courts, pools, or a clubhouse, these are shared.

However, this is also a plus because you have access to these amenities (as well as all other common areas) without having to worry about their upkeep directly. The same holds true typically for front yards and sometimes back and even side yards, which are kept up by the home owners' association. However, a detracting feature is that there is usually a monthly dues assessment which pays for all that upkeep. This monthly fee typically ranges from $150 to $300, a not unlarge sum.

Townhouses, which are generally defined as allowing you the ownership of the ground beneath and the air above, can be a happy compromise for some. They generally offer lower density (compared to condo and co-ops where you may have other owners above and below as well as around you). They may also offer private patios and larger garages.

Some more recent single-family detached homes are also a bit of a compromise. While you own the home outright, you may also belong to a home owners' association that takes care of all front yards and offers some of the amenities described above. When you throw in a security gate to prevent all but owners from getting in, you add even more privacy. Generally speaking, gated communities command higher prices, perhaps 5 to 7 percent higher if they are condos or townhouses, and sometimes much higher amounts if they are detached homes.

Some of the problems of shared communities include bad homeowners' associations (for example, those with insufficient reserves, which result in sudden, high dues increases, or which get entangled in lawsuits and require you to spend time helping straighten things out). Shared communities may have too many tenants in the development (tenants tend to not take as good care of property as owners).

16. What Features That I Select Now Will Help Me Resell Later On?

The Quick Answer

The old adage is that you make your profit when you buy, not when you sell. What you should look for are those amenities that are usually preferred by the majority of people. These include: a good appearance, a good location on the block, a good school district, a low crime area, and a big enough size to appeal to a wide variety of buyers. Avoid features that only a few people would like, thus limiting your spectrum of potential buyers later on.

The Expanded Answer

Buy with the right features and later on you can sell more quickly and for a greater profit. So, what amenities do most buyers want? Since you're a buyer, you probably have some strong feelings on this subject yourself. However, while you may be right on target in some cases, you could be miles off in others.

Here's a list of some of the most preferred items, not necessarily in order of priority.

1. *Three or four bedrooms.* A two-bedroom home with each being a master bedroom has become popular recently, particularly for families without children. But there are far more buyers with children than without children out there. More bedrooms makes the home more versatile.

2. *Two to three bathrooms.* Some older homes have only one bath, which is considered a detracting feature. Generally, most buyers will subtract the cost of putting in a second bathroom from any price you set. (If you're considering buying a home with a single bathroom, you should do the same thing!)

3. *Two- or three-car garage.* A one-car garage is considered a detracting feature. People prefer bigger garages because homes generally have limited storage space and the garage becomes a great place to store items.

4. *Fireplace and air-conditioning.* These are no longer extras, but are expected in almost all climates. A house without them may sell for less, and it may take much longer to find a buyer.

5. *Family room.* Formal dining rooms are shrinking in size or being eliminated entirely, while family rooms are growing in size. A dining *L* or nook may suffice, but a house without a good size family room is a no-no.

6. *Adequate footage.* At least 1500 but preferably 2000 or more square feet for a house. At least 1200 but prefer-

ably 1500 or more square feet for a condo or town-house.

7. *A large kitchen.* Buyers these days are returning to the old style of a farm kitchen with at least a breakfast nook or eating area inside.

8. *One story instead of two.* Many people don't care, and some prefer two stories, where the bedrooms are upstairs, more secure and more isolated. But the elderly and those with small children can find climbing stairs a burden, and you don't want to limit your potential pool of buyers when you sell.

9. *Insulation.* Energy costs are skyrocketing everywhere and a well-insulated house can keep those costs down. Check for double-pane windows and insulation in walls and under floors as well as in the attic.

17. Should I Buy a Corner Lot? A House with a Pool?

The Quick Answer

Not if you want to avoid problems later on. A corner lot can be a problem selling because you could have noisy traffic on two sides. A pool house may seem desirable, but maintaining a pool, particularly an older one, can present headaches you never dreamed of.

The Expanded Answer

Let's take corner lots first. My advice is to avoid them. Although they are often promoted as a special added feature, they actually can detract from value. The reason is twofold. First, as just noted, you get traffic on two sides of the home. Second, a corner lot means more open area in the front of the house, where it usually is not usable and requires added maintenance. At the same time, because you have an open front on two streets, the size of the backyard is reduced, meaning less privacy.

Pools, on the other hand, generally help sell homes. I personally believe this is because most people have never had a house with a pool and dream of it as a luxury. Pools can be nice, particularly if you have children and are in a mild climate; children tend to enjoy pools immensely.

But pools can be difficult and expensive to maintain. You may need a pool service, particularly if, as noted, the pool is older or has a problem. Plus there is the added liability. You will undoubtedly have to increase your insurance to cover the pool. The old saw here is that the two best days of your life are the day you buy your pool home and the day you sell it.

Think twice before buying a home with the intent of later putting in a pool. These days pools are fabulously expensive to build. What with stricter building code requirements, more expensive materials and labor, $20,000 for even a small pool is not unreasonable. And when it comes time to sell, you probably won't get even half that amount back.

A possible alternative is the spa. The spa was originally popularized as a "hot tub" on the West Coast, but then the idea moved across the country. It is essentially a small pool of hot water, with accompanying air and water jets, in which to relax. At one time, spas definitely helped sell homes because they were a fad and it seemed everyone wanted one. In most areas today, however, the popularity has diminished, and buyers can take or leave a spa. As a result, they are considered an attractive feature, but usually don't add anything to the home's price. I wouldn't pay extra for one, but would be pleased to have it thrown in as part of the purchase price. Spas generally require minimal maintenance.

18. Should I Look for FSBO Homes?

The Quick Answer

You may save money, but negotiating the deal will usually be more difficult. The seller of a for sale by owner (FSBO) has not listed the house with an agent, usually to avoid paying a hefty commission. Some agents will not show you FSBOs, so you may need to find them on your own. Sometimes the sellers have cut the price to get a quick sale, so these can be a real bargain. At other times, the sellers may have set an unrealistically high price, and the home may be no bargain at all.

The Expanded Answer

There are both pros and cons in dealing with FSBOs. The pros are usually a lower price. Wise sellers will often reduce the sales price by a large portion of the amount that would otherwise go to paying the agent's commission, and this can save you money. For example, if the listing rate is 6 percent and the house sells for $150,000, that's $9000 in commission. If the sellers reduce the price, say $6000 (keeping the equivalent of $3000 for themselves), that's a hefty savings for the buyer. Besides, savvy buyers can sometimes pressure the seller to reduce the price the equivalent of an entire commission (or more) thus getting a true bargain. This is usually the case only in a slow market.

   The difficulty in buying a FSBO is that you must deal directly with the sellers without the benefit and expertise of an agent. When handling the negotiations, the agent acts as an intermediary, often soothing hurt feelings and at the same time coaxing the price down and getting you better terms. Unless you are a very skilled negotiator, you may find this difficult to do in a face-to-face situation with sellers.

Further, once you and the sellers have agreed upon the price, there's a lot of important paperwork, including disclosures, you must get from the sellers, and there are inspections you must arrange. The agent is, presumably, up-to-date on all of these and can guide you efficiently through the purchase process.

On the other hand, many sellers are just as knowledgeable as agents. The sellers may already have all the paperwork ready to go, can assist with getting inspections and may have an arrangement with a lender to help you get financing!

Sometimes you can buy a FSBO with an agent (thus, getting your cake and eating it too!). Most FSBOs are willing to pay a half commission to any agent who brings them a legitimate buyer. If the listing fees in the area are 5 percent, for example, most FSBOs will pay the agent 2½ percent. Since this is the same amount as the agent would get by being the selling broker for another agent's listing, they are usually quite willing to go along. If you're working with an agent, have the agent call the FSBO and see if they'll pay a selling commission (half). If they are willing to do so, then just have the agent handle the deal for you. You could get the benefit of a lower price *and* the convenience of having a professional do the dirty work!

Overall, buying a FSBO is harder to do than working through an agent, but it is not impossible. If it works for you, the rewards may be worth an extra effort.

19. Should I Consider a Fixer-Upper (Handyman Special)?

The Quick Answer

Yes, if you're a handyperson. In addition to skill, hard work, entrepreneurial spirit, and no little amount of luck, fixer-uppers also usually require extra cash (or access to additional financing). If you're adventuresome, they can allow you to make a purchase in a neighborhood you would otherwise not be able to afford. And you may just be able to resell for a hefty profit. Only remember, the place will be run down when you buy it, and it will be entirely up to you to fix it up.

The Expanded Answer

There are many reasons for buying a fixer-upper, and all of them come down to reduced price. These homes run the gamut from being cosmetically challenged (needing mostly paint and cleaning) to having catastrophic problems (falling down a hillside, underwater, no roof, and so on). What they have in common is that because of their problem (mild to severe), the sellers have reduced the price (a little to a lot). The opportunity is to go in and, using "sweat equity," clean up, fix up and then either live in the property or sell it for a profit.

The real danger with a fixer-upper is that you'll get in over your head. Often tasks that new would-be fixer-upper people think they can do by themselves, such as plumbing, gas line repair, electrical connections, plastering, and so on, turn out to be far more complicated and difficult than they anticipated. They may need to call in professional help not only to do the original job, but to undo the botched work they originally did. The cost can be very high and can turn a real bargain into a very real nightmare. (If you want a clear example of what can go very, very wrong in such a case, rent the movies *Pacific Heights* and *The Money Pit* out of your neighborhood video rental store. I recommend every potential fixer-upper see these!)

Additionally, many of those new to real estate fail to realize that it's difficult to get financing once you've begun remodeling. Either you must have enough cash on hand to see the work through, or you must have made arrangements beforehand, usually at the time of the purchase.

The real trick to successfully doing fixer-uppers is to first know your own skills and limitations and second use a very sharp pencil when calculating how much to pay. This usually involves doing some backward calculations. To arrive at the correct purchase price, begin by estimating the ultimate price you will be able to resell the property for, then subtract all of the costs of refurbishing plus costs of purchase and sale. That's how much you should pay. You may find that you need to pay a lot less than you think in order to make a profit, or even come out even.

For more information on buying fixer-uppers, consult my book *The Home Remodeling Organizer* (Dearborn, 1995).

20. What Should I Look for When I Tour a Home?

The Quick Answer

Look at the location: Is it in the school district you want? Is the neighborhood safe? Is there easy access to freeways or rapid transit? Look at the size: Are there enough bedrooms and are they big enough? Are the kitchen and the family room big enough for you? Is the garage big enough, with enough storage space? Look at the condition: Are the bathrooms and kitchen modern or remodeled? Look at the floor plan: Will it work for you? Avoid looking at the furniture.

The Expanded Answer

You need to exercise your imagination, something sorely lacking in too many buyers. You need to see the home as it will look when you're living in it with your furniture, not as it is now with the sellers things. That may mean overlooking the green wallpaper and the purple carpets—perhaps you'll repaint and recarpet (and price your offer accordingly!). Look for items that appeal to you in a home—an eating area in the kitchen, a fireplace in the master bedroom, a large or small back yard.

Be very careful when judging size. Too often a large room can be made to look small by being cluttered with furniture. Conversely, a truly small area can appear larger than it is when it is empty and when floor-to-ceiling mirrors are installed on one or more walls.

My suggestion is that the first time through you spend your efforts looking for the positive. Try to find a reason why you would want to live in this house.

Don't be hesitant about poking around. If there are throw rugs on the floor, feel free to lift up a corner to see what the flooring underneath is like. If there's a pantry off the kitchen, open the door and walk into it to judge its size. If there's a separate area in the master bath for a toilet, shower or other fixture, walk into the area and see whether it's truly big enough or whether it's cramped. Try the garage door opener. Walk to the back of the lot. See the whole property.

Then, after you leave, if you really like the property, go back and see it a second time. *Never make an offer on a property you haven't seen at least twice.* On the second visit look for the negatives. Is the front door loose on its hinges? What about the paint inside and out—is it in good, fair, or poor condition? What about the roof and the carpeting? Are the appliances new and in good, clean shape? Do the air conditioning and heating work? (Don't hesitate to try them out.) Are the windows adequate (double pane, well located in rooms to let in lots of light)? Are there screens on all windows and outside doors? Is the basement wet or damp?

If there are obvious defects, you may want to pass or lower your offer accordingly. If you decide to buy, be sure to add a contingency in the sales agreement that allows you a certain number of days (usually 10 days) to have the property inspected by a professional. If more defects turn up, you can ask the seller to fix them or reduce the price. (See Chapter 9 for more on this strategy.)

21. How Many Houses Should I See in One Day?

The Quick Answer

It depends on your stamina and ability to recall what you've seen. Agents can sometimes look at 20 or more homes in a day and easily remember the price, terms, and features of each. Home buyers, on the other hand, particularly those who are just beginning to look, may find that just half a dozen is the maximum. What's important is that you don't get overly tired and saturated with looking to the point where everything blends together. You could miss the perfect home!

The Expanded Answer

It's very helpful if you take along a pad and make notes as you go through each house. List those features that you like and those that you dislike. Savvy agents will usually prepare a printout of the features of each home you are going to see and give it to you so you can write notes on the back. Some really professional agents will bind together all of the printouts into a small booklet so that you can keep them together for easy reference. They may even try to show you the properties in the order they appear in the booklet to help you remember.

In addition, these days most sellers (or their agents) will prepare a flyer that you can pick up at the house that offers a picture and a list of the home's better features and gives its price as well as any special terms. The picture is particularly helpful in recalling a home later on. One agent I know takes along a Polaroid camera and shoots a few pictures of each house to give to her clients to help them remember. There's nothing to keep you from taking along your own camera for the same purpose.

If you have created a "wants list," as suggested in question 14 in this chapter, bring it along and compare it to each house as you go through or afterward, sitting in your or the agent's car. I can remember going with buyers on several occasions who did this and sometimes were surprised to realize that the house they had just seen fitted most of their requirements, even though they didn't realize that when they were walking through. (It works conversely, too. You may fall in love with a brick fireplace, but a check with your "wants list" may quickly show the house definitely isn't for you.)

One thing I have found particularly helpful is to have the agent prepare a map of the area with each house you see (or you can do it yourself). You can list them as 1, 2, 3 or A, B, C or whatever so that the location on the map corresponds to the printout of the homes seen. I find this very helpful in recalling where I've been and what I've viewed. *And,* if I want to go back later on for a second look at the neighborhood by myself without the agent, I don't have trouble finding the house.

Finally, don't walk through silently. Speak up. Talk to your spouse, friend, agent, or whomever you go with. Point out what you like and dislike. Just saying it out loud helps fix it in your memory.

22. Should I Try to Buy the Seller's Furniture?

The Quick Answer

Probably not. Sometimes buyers will make an offer which includes the seller's furniture. Often times this will be for more than the asking price, to accommodate the furniture's cost. Usually, but not always, this is a mistake. If a seller has a good eye, the furnishings may make the place ever so appealing. But looking to the furniture instead of the home can be a costly error. The furniture will be old and worn out in a few years and, unless it's truly antique, will be virtually worthless. The home alone, however, if well bought, will appreciate in value.

The Expanded Answer

I've seen deals where the buyers have made the purchase contingent on the furniture being thrown in and then offered less than full price, but not much less. For example, a friend recently bought a home in Scottsdale, Arizona. It was marvelously decorated in a Southwest decor. The buyers asked the sellers if they would consider selling the furniture. The sellers said they would, but wanted $10,000 extra for it.

My friends checked out the market and felt the home was fairly priced. They then made an offer for slightly below full price, cash to a new loan, and included the furniture. The sellers wanted to sell, considered the cost of moving the furniture across the country to Maine, where they were going (and where the decor might not fit), and simply agreed. It was easier to just move on.

What's important to note here is that the offer my friends made was for the market price, or close to it. Yes, they might have forced the sellers to lower the price a bit more, but then my friends would have had to go out and spend around $10,000 on furniture. This way they got the house at a fair price (one they might have paid for a similar home without any furniture thrown in), *plus* they got a house full of furnishings. Sometimes, not always, it does work out.

Be wary of mixing personal property (furniture) with real property (the home) on the purchase agreement when you buy. It can be confusing to both you and the sellers and can mask the true value of the property as far as the lender is concerned. If personal property is included in the sales agreement, lenders may think the purchase price is based in part on furniture (which it may be). Since they are making a real estate mortgage, not a chattel (furniture or other personal property) loan, they may lower the amount they are willing to give accordingly. Sometimes a side agreement to buy the furniture works best in this situation.

23. How Do I Know If I Can Afford to Buy a Home?

The Quick Answer

You or any good real estate agent can quickly determine your mortgage, tax, and home owners' insurance monthly payment. You can add in a logical amount for utilities. Don't forget to include something for maintenance and repair, more if the house is older. This should be your total housing cost. If it's a third of your gross income, you're probably okay, although some few people can manage when it's as much as half.

The Expanded Answer

Chances are that in order to get a home, you're going to have to obtain financing for between 80 and 90 percent of the purchase price. As part of the financing process, the lender will secure a credit report on you as well as confirmation of your income and expenses and an estimate of all the costs noted above. The lender, using profiles established after analyzing hundreds of thousands of similar borrowers, will grant you the loan only if it thinks you can afford to make the payments. While this does not guarantee you can afford the house, if a lender says you can, it's usually something you can bank on.

For first-time buyers the real issue here is often "sticker shock." The costs of home ownership can sometimes be double the costs of renting. In a panic such buyers sometimes feel, "I can't possibly make those kinds of payments!" Usually it takes several months of successfully making all the payments before we calm down and feel more secure in our investment.

And remember, while it almost always does cost more to own a home, it's important to consider that there are certain trade-offs. Up to certain very high limits, you can usually deduct your mortgage interest, which typically is the major portion of your mortgage payment (at least initially) from your income taxes. You can also deduct your property taxes. These two deductions can be very substantial, often in many thousands of dollars. They mean that you will owe less in income taxes at the end of the year, sometimes a lot less. Have your accountant make the exact calculation for you. If this is your first home and you haven't claimed these deductions before, you may be able to claim more personal deductions and increase your take-home pay significantly. As a result, though the house costs a lot more, owning it may actually increase your spendable income!

Of course, it is possible to get in over your head. This is particularly the case when buyers use some sort of "creative financing," where they put very little down and have a whole series of mortgages, from an institutional lender, from a seller, and from third parties. Always keep in mind that there's a price to pay for everything, although that price may not be evident at first. Usually the price for putting less of a down payment into a property is much higher payments.

24. Should I Be Concerned about the Home Owners' Association?

The Quick Answer

Yes, absolutely! The single biggest cause of lawsuits involving property ownership today probably revolves around home owners' associations (HOAs). The HOA is run by its members, and it could be badly run. You should carefully check out the HOA, if your property has one, before you buy. A red flag is existing and/or past law suits. Also, see if the HOA has enough in reserve to pay for scheduled maintenance, such as roof replacement and painting. And ask existing owners if there are problems with the HOA not otherwise evident.

The Expanded Answer

All condominiums and townhouses belong to a HOA. A co-op has a similar arrangement and some single-family detached homes belong to HOAs as well. If you are buying in any sort of a planned development or community, chances are the home will have a HOA. Be sure to ask to see the bylaws, and the covenants, conditions, and restrictions (CC&Rs), as well as any other pertinent information.

The HOA takes care of all property owned in common. This often includes walking paths, grounds, and amenities such as swimming pools, spas, and recreation rooms. It often will also be responsible for the outside maintenance of the building, including roof, walls, fences, and so on.

Most buyers are unpleasantly surprised by the monthly dues when they first buy a home that belongs to a HOA. Today these dues can frequently be between $150 and $300 a month. That is a substantial amount and particularly daunting when added to a mortgage, tax, and insurance payment. As a consequence, I have had buyers ask if they could withdraw from the HOA—do any upkeep and so on themselves—and not pay the monthly dues.

Unfortunately, that is not possible, unless all of the other HOA members agree, which is most unlikely. The HOA normally comes with the property and is included in the CC&Rs, which lists just what it says.

However, even though the dues may be high, be aware that you often get value for your money. You probably won't have to pay much, if anything, for outside upkeep. And the HOA may additionally pay for fire, flood, or earthquake insurance. In other words, much of the money you pay in HOA dues may come back to you in benefits.

As noted, beware of bad HOAs. Boards composed of home owner members run these associations, and sometimes things don't work out very well. Some members become so angry at what they consider unfair decisions that they won't talk to each other for years. I have seen actual fist fights break out at HOA meetings! Usually you can determine how well run your HOA is by checking for old and pending lawsuits, as noted above. Also, as noted, take the time to ask some neighbors. Often they can and will give you the lowdown.

Additionally, you may want someone experienced with HOAs, an attorney or accountant, to check out their books to see how financially solid they are.

Finally, you are entitled to see all HOA documents that affect your home before you buy. Insist on seeing them. If the sellers or HOA cannot make them reasonably available, that in itself is a very bad sign.

3

How Do I Judge a Neighborhood?

25. What Does "Location, Location, Location!" Really Mean?

The Quick Answer

It means that the most important determiner of property value is where the home is. Take a brand-new house (the building alone) that costs $100,000 and put it in the best section of town and it may sell for $300,000. Put it in the worst section of town and it may sell for barely its $100,000 construction cost. Further, well-located property will sell quicker and appreciate faster in value. Poorly located property may take forever to sell and actually decline in value! In real estate, the most important consideration is where it is, not what it is.

The Expanded Answer

The question really is asking, what determines location, more precisely, good location?

Location actually is composed of many factors, each of which should be carefully considered before buying a home. These include:

Proximity to good or bad influences (A good influence could be a college or a lake; a bad influence might be high-voltage power lines overhead or a toxic dump site.)

Quality of Schools (This is a very important location factor, which is discussed in greater detail in the next section.)

The amount of crime in the area (This is another very important location factor, which is also discussed in the next section.)

Nearby shopping (Most owners don't like to drive long distances for necessities or even for extras.)

Easy access to freeways or rapid transit lines (This is very important because most people work long distances away from home.)

Appearance (How does the home look, including landscaping and cleanliness?)

Prestige (This is a subtle quality that refers to how others in the community perceive the neighborhood.)

It really doesn't take much effort to find out which are the more desirable areas and which the less. All you need do is go out with an agent for an afternoon. Just ask to see the better areas, and any agent worth his or her salt can show them to you.

Further, you can easily tell for yourself. The better locations simply look better. They aren't run-down. There is pride of ownership evident everywhere.

The trouble, of course, is that the better locations cost more. As a result, many buyers simply cannot afford them and, hence, are forced to look in less affluent locations.

There is nothing wrong with this, as long as you keep at least two things in mind: First, there is a definite trade-off between price and location. You usually get what you pay for. This means that while buying in a less desirable location might not cost as much, chances are the property won't appreciate as fast either and you may not make as much when you sell.

Second, big bargains can sometimes be found in less desirable locations. Neighborhoods rarely remain constant—most are always in a state of flux. If you find a neighborhood that is on the way up (because of a new plant moving in not far away or because people are fixing up their homes), you may be able to buy in cheap and later sell for a whopping profit. But this takes careful analysis and not just a little bit of luck.

26. What Do I Need to Know about Schools and Crime?

The Quick Answer

The ideal is finding a neighborhood with the best schools in the state and virtually no crime whatsoever. (Doesn't exist, many people will say!) The real is that better schools and lower crime rates translate into higher home values. After all, given a choice, wouldn't you opt for the neighborhood with the best schools and lowest crime rate you could afford? You should!

The Expanded Answer

I've made an informal study of neighborhoods in several cities in the Southwest for over 30 years and have come to the conclusion that the single most important factor in determining value that home owners can influence is the quality of schools. Time and again I've seen areas in which the home owners voted for schools bonds, and as a result, saw their homes go up in value. On the other hand, areas which on a regular basis voted down any sort of bonds for schools have tended to stagnate and not increase rapidly in value and, in some cases, actually declined. Put simply, good schools mean good neighborhoods.

On the other hand, I've seen some supposedly savvy buyers check out the tax bill of a property they were considering and be turned off because of a school assessment that showed up. My thinking is the other way around. Neighborhoods willing to vote for better schools reap the rewards down the line in higher home prices. A school tax assessment is a plus when house hunting, not a minus.

You can find out about the quality of the local schools by asking agents. Since this information is requested so often, they usually have the answers. You can also go to the local school district offices and ask to see the results of standardized tests that children take. Look for tests in a range of grades from elementary to high school. The higher the percentile scored, the better the schools. Generally, anything over the 80th percentile is considered good.

Regarding crime, the situation across the country is not encouraging. While as of this writing, crime in most categories seems to be on the decline, burglaries in many areas are still a significant problem. The truth is that no neighborhoods are crime free.

As a result, those that have fewer crimes tend to thrive. This is particularly the case for gated communities. Having the presumed extra security a gate offers, often adds 5 percent or more to the value of the property inside. Once again, you pay more when you buy, but you get more when you sell.

As with schools, agents are a good source of information. Checking at the local police precinct can usually yield some rather precise local crime statistics.

27. Should I "Walk" the Neighborhood?

The Quick Answer

Always! I always believe that before I buy a car, I should take it for a test drive. (After all, how else can I be completely sure that it actually works?!) Similarly, I believe that before buying a home, I should walk the neighborhood, talk to people, see what things look like up close. How else will I gain information on what it's really like and if I'll truly enjoy living there?

The Expanded Answer

You can't tell enough about a neighborhood by simply driving by. You need to get out of the car and spend several hours walking the area. (If you're afraid to walk the area, should you really be buying there?)

Try to time your walk so that it's on the weekend or, if that's not possible, at least later in the afternoon or in the early evening. Besides looking at the condition of other homes and their landscaping, you'll find neighbors out and about.

When you find neighbors, make it a point to speak to them. Explain that you're considering buying a house in the area and ask if they can tell you anything about it. Do they consider it safe? Are there loud teenagers riding around at night? Are there fights or shootings? Is it quiet all the time? Are there any problems?

Most people, once you've explained why you're asking, will be happy to inform you. If you're lucky, you'll chance upon the neighborhood gossip and you'll learn more than you probably care to know!

On your walk also pay special attention to the front yards of the houses. Are the lawns all mowed, the bushes trimmed, everything green and fresh? Or are there weed-strewn yards, is trash blowing around, are broken cars parked on lawns? What you want to determine is whether the neighbors have pride of ownership and are willing to take care of their properties. If they do, it's an excellent sign. Remember, while you might miss an occasional problem house on a driveby, you should see everything when walking. (Be aware that in some areas it is the HOA's responsibility to care for front yards. Bad appearances may not be the home owner's fault, but rather an indication of a bad HOA.)

Also, check out the houses themselves. If they're new, they should all appear in good shape. If they're older, check out the condition of the paint, look for broken windows, doors, and screens. Is everything in good shape, or are lots of the homes drab and run-down? An older area in good shape usually indicates the owners' sense that the neighborhood has strong property values and their willingness to put in the necessary money to keep up their properties, a very good sign.

Finally, if it is an older and run-down neighborhood, are there many homes being rehabbed in the area? This kind of sweat equity work is usually done by younger couples. At least a third and hopefully more than half the homes either being refurbished or already fixed-up usually indicates a neighborhood on the rise. It might be a great opportunity to buy, fix up, and later sell for a hefty profit. Also look into my book *Buy Right, Sell High* (Dearborn, 1997) for more help here.

28. What Should I Ask an Agent about a Neighborhood?

The Quick Answer

The most important question is how likely are the homes to appreciate in value? What you want is an estimate of future value. Keep in mind, however, that agents may know of neighborhoods only by reputation. They may not be aware of specific problems that are brewing that could have a deleterious effect in the future.

The Expanded Answer

You can ask the agents anything about a neighborhood that you want information on. However, in some cases the agents may not know the answers, and in other situations, they may be unable to tell you what they know. For example, you may ask about the racial or ethnic mix in a neighborhood. Agents have to be very careful about not showing (or giving the appearance of showing) any racial or ethnic bias. Therefore, many simply will choose to avoid answering your question.

On the other hand, if you say something like, "I'd like to live in a community that has a large Jewish population," or "I'd like a community with a large Asian population," and then direct the agent to show you only those communities, most agents will comply, if they can.

You can ask the agent about schools, shopping, crime, pollution, access to freeways and rapid transit, and more. Most agents I've seen in action will immediately give answers to all of these questions. However, it's important to regard these answers as guidelines only and then follow up on your own. For example, the agent may reply, "The schools are just wonderful; amongst the best in the city." If schools are important to you (and they should be for future price appreciation), now check them out yourself. Visit or call the local school board to see how the students have performed on standardized testing. (The higher the score, the better—see question 26 in this chapter.)

Sometimes the answers an agent gives are based almost entirely on the area's reputation. The agent may say that this mature neighborhood is renowned for quiet streets and gardenlike settings. If you ask the agent if he or she lives in the area, the answer may be, "No." Has the agent sold any homes in the area in the past 12 months. Again, perhaps, "No." So what is the value of the agent's answer?

Interestingly enough, reputation is a valuable commodity. (In businesses, it can actually be bought and sold.) If a neighborhood is known to be excellent, then that is certainly a good sign. Only it wouldn't hurt to ask another agent to confirm this.

You should ask an agent about any detracting features or problems. Is there a smelly oil plant or toxic dump site nearby that may affect prices? What about future development of additional homes (that will impact schools, roads, and so on) or commercial or industrial sites (that will make residential areas less desirable)? Agents should know the problems, and they owe you complete disclosure. (But if you're serious about a property, conduct your own investigation to be sure.)

Finally, if you're new to an area, beware of a neighborhood that seems wonderful, yet is unbelievably cheap. You usually get what you pay for, and that's certainly the case in terms of location. If the price is too low, look for a problem. Chances are if you dig deep enough, you'll find one.

29. What Should I Ask a Seller about a Neighborhood?

The Quick Answer

Often when visiting a house, particularly for the second or third time, it's good to spend a little while with the sellers, assuming they're home. (It's a good idea to try to show up when they're likely to be at home.) While they will be eager to point out the good features of the neighborhood, be sure to also ask them if there are any problems. Are there lots of children around? Are there any problem kids or bullies? What about the neighbors—any problems there? If you have specific concerns, ask pointed questions. A few minutes spent here can avoid misconceptions and big problems later on.

The Expanded Answer

Sellers usually know the neighborhood better than anyone else (assuming they've been living in the house and not renting it out to tenants). They know if the neighbor on the south side has a drinking problem and often comes home noisy and drunk at three in the morning waking everyone up. They know if the neighbor behind has kids with a rock band which plays loudly at parties every weekend.

The sellers also know if there's an oil refinery five miles away that discharges vile odors into the neighborhood every third day. Or if there's a bunch of hot-rodders or gang members who come through regularly to terrorize the inhabitants.

You're entitled to know this information because it could influence your decision to buy. When you ask the sellers, they should tell you.

It's important to remember that while in the old days (meaning about 10 years ago), the buyer was at great risk from lack of neighborhood knowledge when purchasing, today things are different. Before, buying a home was kind of a grab bag affair in which you really didn't know what you were getting into until you had bought it...and by then it was often too late or too difficult to do anything about it.

A spate of lawsuits by disgruntled buyers, who felt they had been sold a "pig in a poke," aimed at sellers and agents turned things around. Today, it's the buyers who have great protections, if they exercise them by asking questions. Neighborhood influence is one of them.

In most states sellers must now give buyers a fairly detailed disclosure statement which includes listing any neighborhood problems. If, for example, the sellers fail to disclose that there is a noisy neighbor next door, you move in and can't sleep and subsequently find that the old owner had called the police a dozen times about that neighbor, you could have a case for getting the deal rescinded—forcing the seller to take back the property. No smart seller wants to risk that.

Besides asking questions when touring the house, after you get a purchase offer accepted and receive the seller's disclosure statement, read it carefully and formulate other questions. If there are any problems that you don't understand or that are unclear, ask the seller for a further explanation, in writing. Many states allow you a certain period of time (usually 5 to 10 days) in which to disapprove of the seller's disclosures. If you disapprove, you are not usually committed to continuing the purchase. In that case, use this right to your advantage. Although many buyers don't realize it, in many states the disclosure period after the sale is signed is an excellent time for the buyer to ask all sorts of questions that might not have come up earlier.

Don't be afraid to ask questions of the seller. You'll learn a lot. And if the seller refuses to answer, then that in itself could reveal even more.

30. Should I Check with the Local Planning/Building Department?

The Quick Answer

It's a good idea. Often your agent will do this for you, but not usually unless you ask. At the planning department, you want to check the community's master plan, if it has one, and speak to someone about future development of any kind in and around the area. You may learn that a chemical company is planning to build a pesticide plant only two miles from the home you are considering buying. Or that a tract of 2000 homes is scheduled to break ground next winter, putting strain on existing schools and roads and adding competition to the resale market.

The Expanded Answer

Ideally, you should be able to get all the information you need about land use from the seller and the agent. However, either or both may not know, may forget to mention something, or may overlook a little bit here and there. The only way you can be sure is to check it out for yourself.

Checking with the building and planning departments is usually only one trip, since they are most often located next to each other. Dealing with the planning department is usually just a matter of requesting a moment's time of one of the engineers or attendants, then asking some pointed questions about master plans and developments in the area. All the information is public, and you should have no trouble getting access to it.

31. Should I Check Out Access to Transportation and Shopping?

The Quick Answer

Yes, certainly. You want to know important, even vital pieces of information: Exactly how long will it take you to get to and from work? How far is it to grocery shopping or a gas station? What about department and discount stores? In many congested communities today, simply knowing distances doesn't help. You need to know actual travel times to see if the property is well-located for you.

The Expanded Answer

Here's what I suggest you do. After you've decided on a home you like and want, take the time to go to the house and then drive from there to your work during the times you normally would (usually during rush hour). Later, drive back at the time you normally would. Now, how much time did it take? (Alternatively, drive or walk to the mass transit and take the same measurements.)

The times may surprise you, sometimes even shock you. On the West Coast where I live, it isn't unusual for it to take upwards of one to two hours each way to get from home to work or back. Some people actually drive three hours or longer each way!

My suggestion, however, is that to have a good quality of life, you try to find a place closer to your work. You may have to pay more or settle for less, but to spend a third or more of your waking hours going back and forth to work makes little sense to me.

The same applies to shopping of all kinds. You don't really want the shopping to be too close—mixing too much commercial property with residential property often results in reducing residential values. But, you don't want shopping to be too far, either. Of course, only you can be the judge of this.

One mistake that buyers make is to think that they will buy a home that's far away from the necessities and then, later, get a closer job or eventually sell and move closer in. Unless you're fairly sure a job change is coming up soon, closer to home, don't bet on it. It could be years or might never happen. And remember, the costs of selling and buying a home are about 15 percent (see Chapter 2). Once in, you may find you need to sit on a home three to five years or longer before you can sell and breakeven, let alone make a profit. It is best to check out neighborhood access early on.

4

Where Do I Find a Good Lender?

32. Should I Try to Get a Lender's Prepurchase Commitment?

The Quick Answer

It could help you get into a home, particularly if there are other competing buyers who don't have it. It commits a lender to giving you financing up to a maximum amount. Any time buyers can present an offer which demonstrates that they have a lender ready and willing to make a loan, it's sure to impress a seller. After all, from a seller's perspective, it's equivalent to a cash offer. If there are two buyers offering similar price and terms, one with a commitment and one without, which one would you take if you were the seller?

The Expanded Answer

It's important to understand the difference between getting a prepurchase commitment and getting prequalified. Anyone can prequalify you. Your agent, for example, may ask how much money you make, what your expenses are and from that deduce how big a mortgage you can get. You've just been prequalified.

A lender can do much the same thing plus run a credit check. The lender may even issue a letter saying that you are "prequalified." However, all of this doesn't really amount to much because there's no money behind it. The agent isn't going to give you a mortgage and unless the lender says it's committed, neither is it. It's all just opinion, although with a credit check, it's informed opinion and better than nothing.

However, if you go to a lender, usually a mortgage broker, and say you want a prepurchase commitment, it's something else. It may cost you a few dollars for the more thorough effort, but the lender will not only check your credit report, but verify your employment and salary as well as your funds on deposit. In other words, the lender will go through the same motions that it would take if you had already found a house, signed a sales agreement, and needed a loan. (Using "instant mortgage" techniques now available via computer, some lenders can do this in less than three days! The old-fashioned way, however, usually takes upwards of a month.)

Now, the lender can issue a letter of commitment. In it the lender says that it has done the necessary investigation and will loan Jerry and Sherry Smith up to X number of dollars at a certain loan value (for example, 80 or 90 percent of the sales price). This is something you can take to the bank, almost. It's good to remember that you haven't got a mortgage until you actually get it—things can (and infrequently do) go wrong until the mortgage is actually funded.

A letter of commitment should impress any seller. It means you've done your homework. It means that you've got cash in your pocket. It means that the seller shouldn't have too many worries that you can't afford to buy the home. It means that you can beat out other buyers, and sometimes even get better price and terms.

33. Where Do I Find a Mortgage Lender?

The Quick Answer

They are everywhere. Today your best source of real estate financing is probably the mortgage broker. This is an individual or company that retails mortgages for a variety of lenders including banks, savings and loans, and mortgage bankers. When you go to a mortgage broker, you may be able to select from dozens of lenders, perhaps a hundred different lenders. Mortgage brokers are listed as such in the yellow pages of your phone book. Often real estate agents can recommend mortgage brokers with whom they've had success.

The Expanded Answer

Your choices of a mortgage lender include banks, savings and loans, some credit unions, and mortgage brokers. In the old days you would have to trek from one to another to find the best rates and terms offered. Today, however, most lenders, such as banks (while still offering mortgages to walk-in customers), generally wholesale the mortgages out to mortgage brokers who, in turn, offer them (retail) to the general public. A good mortgage broker will represent the major banks in your area plus be able to offer loans from out-of-state lenders as well as some insurance companies.

It's important to note that a mortgage broker does not actually provide the money. He or she simply acts as a conduit between you and the lender. A mortgage banker, a bank, or a savings and loan, on the other hand, is a true lender that actually funds the mortgage.

Another distinction to remember is between "conforming" and "nonconforming" loans. A *conforming mortgage* is one that your lender will later sell to Freddie Mac or Fannie Mae, the country's two large semigovernmental home-lending agencies. These loans are given this name because they conform to the Freddie Mac/Fannie Mae underwriting guidelines. They currently have a maximum amount of $214,600, but are adjusted up every so often.

A *nonconforming loan* is usually one that is larger or differs in some way from a conforming loan. An example is a "jumbo" mortgage, one that is higher than the current maximum limits on conforming loans. Private lenders, such as banks, offer these larger jumbo loans at a slightly higher interest rate and then carry the mortgage themselves. (These are called *portfolio loans* because they become part of the bank's portfolio, as opposed to being sold to other lenders.)

A good mortgage broker can offer you both conforming and nonconforming loans.

It is important to understand that the amount you pay for a mortgage includes the interest plus the points and fees charged up front. (A point is equal to 1 percent of the mortgage—2 points on a $100,000 loan is $2000.) Normally, whether you go directly to a lender, such as a bank, or a retailer, such as a mortgage broker, the cost, including points and fees, is the same. Even though the lender saves money when you borrow directly, it will not usually pass the savings on to you. To do so would be to undercut its wholesale business, and no lender would do that for the sake of a single mortgage. Thus you won't normally save any money by going directly to a bank instead of dealing with a mortgage broker.

34. How Do I Check Out a Lender?

The Quick Answer

Not all lenders are equal (although all will say they lend equally to anyone who comes through their doors). Most mortgage brokers (and other lenders) are competitive and will offer you a good deal. Some few others, however, will try to get you to pay more. If you are unaware, you can pay unnecessary fees, higher points, or a higher interest rate. The only realistic way to check out a lender is by comparison shopping. After you've talked with a couple of lenders, you'll quickly come to realize what are honest charges and what are not.

The Expanded Answer

The most treacherous time to deal with a lender is when interest rates are particularly low and there are lots of buyers seeking new loans and owners seeking to refinance. At such times it is actually difficult to get a lender's attention simply because so many people are applying for mortgages. Some conniving mortgage brokers realize that it is possible to take advantage of consumers in their frantic efforts to get mortgages while rates are low.

Practices that I have seen which I would label unsavory include:

- *Charging an up-front fee.* This can sometimes be as high as several thousand dollars to process the mortgage. Go elsewhere if a mortgage broker or other lender wants an up-front fee, even if they promise to later credit the fee toward your mortgage costs. (Crediting the fee means that you're tied into the retailer and can't effectively shop elsewhere for better terms.) The only up-front fee you should be charged is for a credit report, which is usually around $35; later there will be a charge for an appraisal, which is around $300 or less.

- *Charging add-on points.* The actual lender (the one who funds the mortgage) may charge points to make up for a lower-than-market interest rate. For example, the market rate might be 8 percent, but the lender is offering 7¾ percent plus 1.5 points. This is a common industry practice. A mortgage broker who is unscrupulous, however, might charge you 2.5 points, pocketing the extra point. Comparison shop to make sure you don't pay too much.

- *Charging garbage fees.* There are some legitimate costs in securing a mortgage, including the fee for a credit report, an appraisal, the points noted above, and some others. Many other charges, such as "document fees" in excess of $50, "processing fees," "preparation fees," and so forth, often adding up to many hundreds of dollars are nothing more than padding. When you pay these fees, they go into the retailer's pocket—the lender doesn't get them, and they don't benefit you. Again, comparison shop the mortgage brokers. You'll quickly discover who is charging extra for no extra service.

- *Charging higher interest rates.* This is rare simply because interest rates are published daily in most newspapers and are widely advertised. However, sometimes the actual interest rate is difficult to determine (such as when you get a "teaser rate" with an adjustable mortgage discussed in question 37). However, after shopping around a bit, you should quickly discover what the market interest rates really are by comparing the annual percentage rate (APR).

35. What Should I Tell the Lender?

The Quick Answer

You will have to bare your most personal financial information to the lender. Be prepared to tell all. Lenders will want to know about every late payment, every debt, and how much money (and other assets) you have and where it is. It's important not to hold anything back, because lenders use sophisticated credit checks to find out. It's better to admit a problem, and explain it with a letter, than try to hide it. If a lender is going to loan you $100,000 or more, it wants to be sure that you have the wherewithal to repay as well as the ethics to do so.

The Expanded Answer

An old rule firmly believed by most lenders is that everyone has perfect credit, until the credit report comes in. The truth is that most of us have a few problems and we know about them. However, we are hoping that these problems won't be picked up.

When you first apply for a mortgage commitment, as noted earlier, a simple credit check will usually be run through a local credit-checking agency. Prior to actually funding, however, the mortgage broker will run a three-agency check. This includes getting a rundown on your credit from EquiFAx, TransUnion, and TRW, the nation's three largest credit-checking agencies. If you have any credit problems, history of late payments, defaults, bankruptcies, or foreclosures, almost certainly they will show up here. In other words, you can run, but you can't hide.

If you have a problem, you can sometimes justify your actions. There was a hurricane that blew down your last home and destroyed your place of work. You had no place to live and were out of work for six months.

Naturally, you didn't make your mortgage payments and went into foreclosure. If the facts are indeed true, a lender-broker may be understanding, particularly if you later picked up the payments or worked out a deal with your old lender.

Don't make up excuses, but if you have a reasonable excuse, tell the lender. It could mean the difference between a "yes" or a "no" in securing the mortgage.

36. Should I Look First for a Low Interest Rate or for Low Payments?

The Quick Answer

There is a direct relationship between the two. The higher the interest rate, the higher the payment and vice versa. Just keep in mind, however, that the payment is based on the actual interest rate charged on the mortgage, not the APR, which takes into account points and fees you have paid and, therefore, is usually higher. For example, the mortgage rate (on which the monthly payment is based) may be 7.5 percent, but the APR (including points and other costs) might be 8 percent. Be sure you calculate your monthly payment here at the 7.5 percent rate.

The Expanded Answer

Most buyers aren't really concerned about the interest rate. They want lower payments. Find a way to get the payment lower and they will opt for it, even if it somehow includes a higher interest rate!

Is that possible? Consider the adjustable-rate mortgage (ARM), which is discussed in greater detail in question 37). ARMs typically have a "teaser" rate, a low initial interest rate. For example, the rate might be 4 percent when the market rate is 8 percent. This means that your payments will be half of those for a fixed-rate (at-market) mortgage. Some buyers jump at this.

The trouble is that typically this introductory rate is for a short time only, perhaps only a month or two. Then, very quickly, the interest rate (and the payments) rise to market rate or higher. It's a case of being pennywise and pound foolish, of going for a lower monthly payment for a few months only to get a higher interest rate and payment later on. (This is a good strategy, on the other hand, if you only plan to own the property a very short while.)

Another danger is "capped" monthly payments, also offered on some ARMs. Here the monthly payment cannot rise beyond a certain point even if interest rates go higher (and should require a higher monthly payment). The trouble is that the interest not paid because of the artificially kept low monthly payments is added to the mortgage, up to 125 percent of the amount initially borrowed. Thus, while the payments are kept low, the amount you owe grows and you end up paying interest on interest!

Pay attention to both the interest rate and the monthly payment. Avoid loans that artificially cap the monthly payment. Look for any mortgages that cap the interest rate.

37. What Type of Mortgage Should I Get?

The Quick Answer

There are basically two types of mortgages, adjustable rates and fixed rates, with an almost infinite variety of combinations of these two types. The general rule is that when interest rates are low, lock in the low rate with a fixed-rate mortgage. When interest rates are high, consider an ARM, where the interest rate and payment will go down as interest rates in general fall.

The Expanded Answer

A good mortgage broker can almost always find a mortgage to suit your requirements. A lot will depend on how good (or bad) your credit is, how big a monthly payment you can afford, and how much money you have to put down. Assuming you have good credit and a normal down payment (10 to 20 percent), here are a few of the mortgages you may be able to consider:

- *Fixed rate.* The interest rate and payment are the same for the entire repayment period. You can reduce the interest rate by going for a shorter term, say 15 years instead of the usual 30, but this will increase the payments.

- *Adjustable rate.* The interest rate and monthly payment will go up and down based on a complex formula associated with an interest rate such as the cost of funds to lenders or the change in T-bill rates. As interest rates overall go up, so do your payments. As they fall, your payments fall.

- *Convertible.* This is a combination fixed and adjustable. The rate may be adjustable for several years with your having the option of switching to a fixed rate at a certain time, say years 5 or 7. This combines a lower ARM monthly payment with the possibility of locking in a fixed rate (if you're lucky and rates happen to be low when your locking window is open).

- *Hybrid.* A shorter-term fixed-rate mortgage, say 3, 5, 7, or 10 years in length, with payments based on a 30-year mortgage. When the time is up, the mortgage hasn't been paid off. It usually (but not always) converts to an ARM. The shorter the term, the lower the interest rates.

These have become among the most popular mortgages.

- *Conforming.* A mortgage following the underwriting guidelines of Fannie Mae or Freddie Mac, quasi-governmental, secondary lenders. They usually require top-flight borrowers and have a maximum loan amount, currently $214,600.

- *Portfolio.* Any loan where the lender does not sell the mortgage in the secondary market to lenders such as Fannie Mae or Freddie Mac, but instead keeps it in its own portfolio. These include "jumbos" or loans for more than conforming loans.

- *Combinations.* Also called *piggy backs,* a conforming loan up to $214,600, then a second mortgage for an additional amount, used primarily to reduce the interest rate and payments when purchasing higher-priced properties.

- *Reverse annuity.* These mortgages are just becoming widely available. They are strictly for older people who have a home that is usually paid off free and clear and need income. The lender pays the borrower a monthly amount, and this builds a mortgage against the home. The important thing is to get a guarantee that the money will keep coming and that the house will not be taken away no matter how long the borrowers live.

- *FHA/VA.* These loans are made by the regular lenders, but because the government, either the Federal Housing Administration (FHA) or the Veterans Administration (VA), insures (in the case of FHA) or guarantees (in the case of VA) repayment, there is a much-reduced down payment (no down payment in the case of VA loans). Requirements are strict and in the case of the VA, require service in the armed forces. Check with a local lender, such as a bank, the

Department of Housing and Urban Development (HUD), or the Veterans Administration, to find out if you qualify.

38. Should I Put More or Less Money Down?

The Quick Answer

The general rule when investing is to put as little of your own money into a project as you can. In that way you reduce your risk and maximize your profit. For example, if you put $40,000 into a home and later sell for a $10,000 profit, you've made 25 percent on your money. If you put $10,000 into the same home and sell for a $10,000 profit, you've made 100 percent on your money!) However, you may not have a choice. You may need to put a lot of money down if you have poor credit or in order to reduce your monthly payment.

The Expanded Answer

In the old days lenders required a certain minimum down payment, typically 20 percent, in order to grant you a mortgage. They felt that if a borrower didn't put at least 20 percent down, that borrower might not make the monthly payments.

Recent statistical studies, however, have shown that the amount of money put down has far less to do with repaying the mortgage than the overall credit profile of the borrower. Some borrowers always repay debt, others are forever late payers and defaulters. Thus lenders today have come up with a better way of determining who will repay and who won't. They have created computer profiles. Based on your past credit history, you can now put down as little as 10 percent or 5 percent or, in some trial cases, nothing! However, the lower the down payment, the better your credit must be. Any good mortgage broker can steer you in the right direction here.

On the other hand, the less you put down, the bigger the mortgage and the monthly payments. Some borrower/buyers, particularly those who have just sold a home and received a substantial amount of cash for their old equity, will put extra money down, sometimes a third or half of the price of their new home. The reason is to get those payments down. If you buy a home for $200,000 and put $10,000 down (5 percent) at 9 percent interest over 30 years, the payments are $1529 a month. If you are able to put $100,000 down at the same interest rate, you can cut those payments almost in half to $841.

However, keep in mind that the more you put down, the more money you are tying up that can't be spent or invested elsewhere. If you could otherwise put that down payment in a CD and earn 5 percent interest on it, that's $5000 per $100,000 annually that your money's not earning by being tied up in a house. Own the house for five years and you've lost $25,000 in interest you could have otherwise received on the money. The only way you can recoup is if you can resell for a strong profit. This, as the real estate recession of the early 1990s has shown, is no longer a guarantee.

39. What Is PMI Insurance and Do I Need It?

The Quick Answer

When you get an institutional mortgage (a conforming loan or one from a bank, savings and loan, or similar institution) and *put less than 20 percent down,* you may be required to get private mortgage insurance (PMI) to cover the mortgage. The insurance doesn't cover you—it covers the lender in case you default. The cost of the insurance varies but is typically around one-half of 1 percent. In other words, add about half a percent to the interest rate on which you calculate your monthly payments.

The Expanded Answer

The insurance actually covers only the difference between the amount of your mortgage and 80 percent of the value of the property. For example, if you put down 10 percent and got a 90 percent mortgage, the insurance covers the 10 percent difference between 90 percent of value and 80 percent of value. This protects lenders of high "loan-to-value mortgages."

The real issue is what happens after you've owned the property for a while and either have paid down the mortgage or the property value has increased to the point where the loan-to-value ratio is now 80 percent or less? (The loan is 80 percent or less of the property's value.) In theory you should be able to cancel the PMI insurance and save the extra amount you're paying monthly.

However, lenders in general have been lax about informing borrowers when this happens. And some few unscrupulous lenders have even canceled the PMI insurance, not informed borrowers, and kept taking the extra premiums paid by borrowers, keeping it for themselves! Federal regulations to govern PMI have been promised, but are not law as of this writing.

Before trying to have your PMI insurance canceled, you should first be sure you don't confuse PMI insurance with some other type of insurance such as home warranty or life. PMI can and should be canceled when your mortgage loan-to-value ratio drops to 80 percent or less.

To do it, call your lender. That's the easy part. The lender may then require you to jump through a series of hoops, including having a new appraisal. This can cost several hundred dollars, but may be worth it. Dropping the PMI insurance might save you a hundred dollars a month or more on payments, depending on the size of your mortgage!

PMI insurance is a nuisance for many borrowers (about five million home owners currently carry it). But, if you're putting less down, you may not have a choice.

40. What Are Points and How Many Must I Pay?

The Quick Answer

A point is equal to 1 percent of the mortgage borrowed. If you borrow $150,000 and pay one point, it is $1500. Three points on a $100,000 mortgage are $3000. The lender determines the points you must pay, but these are somewhat negotiable. If you pay a higher interest rate, you can reduce the points. A lower interest rate can result in more points.

The Expanded Answer

Points are used in many areas of finance to reconcile a loan's yield with the market rate. For example, the market interest rate might currently be 8 percent. But, in the competitive world of real estate finance, lenders are offering mortgages to borrowers for 7¾ percent, ¼ percent below market.

Logically speaking, however, how can a lender offer a mortgage for less than market? It would mean a loss for the lender. Hence, lenders charge additional money up front to make up for that ¼ percent loss in interest. They might charge two points. (The actual amount is a function of the yield of the loan which combines several factors including interest rate, points, and other fees.) In other words, two points plus $7\frac{3}{4}$ percent interest might be equal to 8 percent and no points for the lender.

Can you opt for a "no-points mortgage"? With some lenders you can. They will give you a sliding scale of interest rate versus points. In our example, an interest rate of $7\frac{7}{8}$ percent might require one point; a rate of $7\frac{5}{8}$ might require three points.

$7\frac{5}{8}\%$	3 points
$7\frac{3}{4}\%$	2 points
$7\frac{7}{8}\%$	1 point
8%	0 points (market rate)

You, as the borrower, need to decide what's more important to you. Points represent cash out of your pocket up front at the time of purchase. A higher interest rate represents a higher monthly payment. The trade-off, therefore, is between cash up front or higher monthly payments. Pay more points and you'll have lower monthly payments. Accept higher monthly payments, and you'll need less cash up front.

Does this mean that the interest rates charged by all lenders are essentially the same, that the only difference is the number of points charged to lower the rate below market? Yes and no. There is also a time factor. Lenders obtain commitments for funds at different times, and these last for anywhere from 30 days to 90 days or longer. As a result, some lenders may be able to loan money at what the interest rate was three months ago, perhaps lower or higher than today. Overall, however, except in a very volatile market, the rates usually are very similar.

Note: When buying a home, some points may be deductible from your taxes. Check with your accountant.

41. What If the Lender Rejects My Application?

The Quick Answer

If you're dealing with a good mortgage broker, this almost never happens today. The reason is that mortgage brokers work with a wide variety of lenders and usually there is some lender somewhere who will offer you a mortgage, no matter what your past financial history is like. It may be for a higher interest rate, for more points, or for a lesser amount than you want, but virtually everyone can get some kind of mortgage today. If you're dealing with a bank or savings and loan that flat out refuses you, go see a good mortgage broker.

The Expanded Answer

Lenders look for prime borrowers. A prime borrower is one who has a long history of having borrowed money, who always made payments on time, and who always repaid debt. If you want a conforming loan (usually those with the best terms) and plan to put the minimum down (only 5 or 10 percent), you'll need impeccable credit, no late payments, not too much credit card debt, and lots of money in reserve. On the other hand, if you're not prime, you can still get a conforming loan by putting more money down. Put down 20 percent and you'll be allowed a little bad credit. Put down 25 percent and you'll be allowed a surprising amount of poor credit history. (Of course, you still can't have had a foreclosure in your past, recent defaults on loans, or lots of very recent late payments).

On the other hand, if you have absolutely terrible credit (never repaid a loan), there are equity lenders who will be happy to lend you money based just on the property's appraised value. There are no borrower qualifications at all! Typically they will loan you 60 to 70 percent of the market value of the property often at a higher interest rate. These lenders don't care if you don't repay, since part of their business is foreclosing and reselling to recoup that big 30 to 40 percent they require you to put down. A good mortgage broker can either get an equity loan for you or recommend you to such a lender. Equity lenders also advertise directly under *mortgages* in the yellow pages of the phone book.

Sometimes you can get an equity loan and still put less down by getting a second mortgage as well, perhaps from the seller or another lender. By combining two loans you may still be able to buy with little money down and with terrible credit!

Finally, in some cases you can assume an existing old FHA or VA loan (those issued many years ago don't require that you qualify in order to assume them). Of course, since they were issued years ago, they are usually for relatively small amounts and require a large down payment (or additional second mortgage financing).

Unlike in the past, in today's real estate market, there is a mortgage for virtually every borrower. Yes, bad credit could cost you in terms of a higher interest rate or more points, but the rate differential between a prime loan and a mortgage to the worst buyer is usually small. The worst borrower may pay only 3 or 4 percentage points more than the best.

Don't accept "No" for an answer. Find another lender/mortgage broker who will say, "Yes."

42. What Do I Do If I Have to Sell My Old Home in Order to Buy, but I'm "Upside-Down"?

The Quick Answer

Being *upside down* means that you owe more on your home than it's worth. This happens during a real estate recession when property values plummet but mortgage balances remain high. If you need to sell in order to buy, but can't, there are only three solutions: Stay and pay, hoping the market will eventually turn around. Pay to sell, where you actually come up with cash to pay down the existing mortgage to a point where it's below the property's value. Work with the lender in a *short sale*, where the lender accepts less than full value for the mortgage. (I don't accept "cut and run" as an alternative, as we'll see shortly. However, as another option you might consider not selling but instead renting out your old house and then buying another with a minimum down payment.)

The Expanded Answer

The best answer, if you must sell to buy, is the short sale. Here the lender accepts less than is owed. The tricky part, of course, is to get the lender to go along.

Most lenders tend to be hard-nosed about such things. If the mortgage document says they are owed, for example, $150,000, but you argue that the house is now only worth $140,000, they may turn a deaf ear. This is particularly the case if you are the sort with excellent credit who always pays on time. They may stonewall, figuring why should they worry when you are so conscientious?

On the other hand, if you haven't made a payment for three months, are planning to pack up and let the house go to foreclosure and to leave the place in a mess, and offer the lender the option of a short sale to get rid of the mortgage without the hassle of foreclosure, most lenders (not all, but most) will tend to be more reasonable. The last thing lenders want is to foreclose. They are in the money-lending business, not the house-fixing and reselling business. Give them a viable option and most will take it.

But, as I said, it's tricky. You need to convince the lender that the short sale is the best option, but at the same time not ruin your own credit to the point where you can't get financing on the new home you wish to buy. In most cases, you'll probably have to tolerate a few months of not making payments, even going so far as to having a "notice of default" filed which indicates you are being foreclosed upon. However, if this shortly has a happy ending, a buyer comes along, and the lender accepts a short sale, a letter of explanation, emphasizing that you were able to sell a house in a bad market, should help when getting that new loan.

What you need to avoid at all costs is walking away (losing the house through foreclosure) when you are upside-down. Cutting and running will be reported to credit companies, and it will haunt you. It almost certainly means that no institutional lender will give you mortgage money for a long time to come. Real estate lenders have long memories, and they fear that what you did to one of their brethren, you may also do to them.

43. Can I Borrow the Down Payment?

The Quick Answer

You're not supposed to. But you might get away with it if you borrow the needed down payment money long before you apply for a new mortgage.

The Expanded Answer

The whole purpose behind a down payment is to be sure that you, the borrower, put some of your own money into the property you are buying. The theory is that you are far less likely to default (not make the payments and lose the property through foreclosure) if you have your own funds at stake.

If you borrow the money, you defeat the whole purpose of the down payment. Borrowing means that all of the money (or a greater percentage than is intended by the lender) is not your own.

When you apply for a mortgage, one of the questions on the application asks where you are getting the money for the down payment. The correct answers are savings, a CD, from liquidating stock, from the sale of other real estate, and so on. The wrong answers are borrowing on credit cards, a loan on other property, a bank line of credit, and so on. Lenders will penalize you severely for borrowing the down payment. In the case of some government-insured loans, it can mean a certain turndown.

Does that mean you can't borrow the down payment? Not necessarily. It just means you must plan carefully.

If you're planning to buy a home and don't have enough cash for the down payment, you may want to borrow it long before you buy, in fact, at least six months earlier. Borrow that money, stick it in the bank, and collect interest on it for six months.

Later when you buy and fill out a mortgage application, you can truthfully say that you didn't borrow the down payment. Rather, you had the money on hand from a loan you took out more than six months ago. If you've been making payments consistently on the money, chances are the lender won't find any problem here.

A word of caution, however. Whenever you borrow, you increase your debt load. Borrowing money that will eventually be used for a down payment may be counterproductive. Yes, you might have the cash. But now your monthly payments (with the additional cost of the borrowed money used for the down payment) might be so high that you can't qualify for the mortgage!

5

How Can I Improve My Credit Report?

44. Should I Order My Own Credit Report Before Looking for a House?

The Quick Answer

It's a good idea. Don't think of credit-reporting companies as infallible. Indeed, they can be very fallible. Mistakes can and do occur, and they often take time, sometimes many months, to correct. That's why checking on your credit early is a good idea.

The Expanded Answer

Remember that old rule in mortgage lending that goes, "Everyone has perfect credit, until the credit report is in."

r credit is spotless, it may turn out
rror made. Or perhaps you really
⁄o years ago that you thought you
ıand, maybe you know that your
ng to be desired. In any event, it
dit check just to be sure. That way
in case there are problems, you can take action early to try
to resolve them.

There are three major credit-reporting companies
nationwide. You can ask any mortgage broker or lender
which of these companies is primarily used in your area,
and then contact them:

Equifax (800) 685-1111

TRW (800) 682-7654

Trans Union (800) 916-8800

You are entitled to a copy of your credit report for a
nominal fee, usually around $8. (If you have been denied
credit, you're entitled to a report for free.) When you get
your report, check it for accuracy. Is your name correct?
Your social security number? Are there any inappropriate
statements of late payment or bad debt.

Don't overlook anything, because you can be sure that
the lender will scrutinize your report. Whatever problems you see will show up to the lender. It is much better
to correct them now, so that when the lender eventually
gets the report, it will be clean.

45. What Can I Do If There Is an Error in My Credit Report?

The Quick Answer

Errors can almost always be cleared up, but it may not be
easy. And it could take several months or, in rare cases,

much longer. The process involves informing the credit-reporting agency of the error and then often going back to the original lender who reported bad credit and getting it to remove its report.

The Expanded Answer

When you get a copy of your credit report, the credit-reporting company will also supply you with information on how to correct any erroneous information. The first step is usually to tell the credit-reporting agency of the problem. You will have to describe the error as clearly as possible. Under the Fair Credit Reporting Act, the credit-reporting agency must investigate your complaint and if it finds an error in its records, correct the error.

If there is no apparent error in its reporting, the credit company will then usually investigate further. Generally speaking this means the credit company will contact the entity that reported the bad credit originally and state that you believe it's in error and ask for a clarification.

If everything goes according to plan, the original reporter of bad debt will discover that you did, in fact, pay back that loan and withdraw the notification of bad credit. Then the credit-reporting company will withdraw the blemish from your credit report. This can happen within 30 days.

In the real world, however, things can be more difficult and take much longer. The original entity reporting bad debt may no longer exist; the company may have gone out of business. Or the records of the company that reported your bad debt may conflict with yours. Even though you paid back a loan, their records show that it is still outstanding. The original lender refuses to withdraw the bad credit complaint.

Or there's something of record (recorded in a county office), such as an erroneous notice of default (part of the foreclosure process), and the credit agency won't remove its notation as long as the notice remains on the county records.

Now you've got some legwork cut out for you. You may have to contact the original loan company and prove to that company (with such things as canceled checks or statements) that you did, in fact, pay the loan off before it will send a note back to the credit-reporting agency removing the bad debt. You may have to get the proper documents from a lender to have the county records amended.

Notice, in all of this, you have to do the work, even though an error may have been made by others. Remember, the credit company just reports; it doesn't act. If it didn't make a mistake in its own files (the bad debt is still claimed by a lender), it usually won't correct it.

In some extreme cases, you may find it next to impossible to get an error removed. In that situation you can ask to have a letter from you explaining the situation included with your credit report. It's not a great solution, but it may be the most practical one in some desperate situations.

46. What If I Always Pay Cash?

The Quick Answer

The only thing worse than bad credit, is no credit. If you always pay cash, you probably don't have any credit record. As a result, a mortgage lender will find it extremely difficult to give you a loan.

The Expanded Answer

Some people are wizards with cash. They don't own and don't want credit cards or loans. They save until they have enough money to buy whatever they need outright.

The problem, here, is that if you're one of these people, you have the next worst thing to terrible credit—you have no credit at all. It's next to impossible to get a home mortgage with no credit. The solution to the problem is to begin establishing credit long before you plan to buy.

The best course of action is to begin establishing your credit at least two years before you plan to buy and obtain a mortgage. You can deposit money in a bank and immediately get a debit card.

Open a checking account. Within a few months of using a checking account, many banks will offer you a credit card. Get it. Once you have one, you will be offered many more from other companies. Get three cards, no more, no less; use the cards and pay them off regularly. (Mortgage lenders usually have a three-card rule. If you have three credit cards, it indicates you have good credit. If you have more than three, it suggests you are abusing your good credit. No, I don't understand it either!)

Next apply for a bank loan. You should be able to use your credit cards to demonstrate enough credit to get it. Then pay it back. Voilà, you have a credit history!

If you don't have two years to play around, here are some shortcuts:

- If you pay water, electric, gas, garbage, or cable bills, chances are you have a check record. (Cash may mean you just don't use credit, not that you don't bank.) Produce your canceled checks along with statements to show that you pay on time. Even if you pay with actual cash, get a letter from the utility company testifying to your prompt payment.

- If you're renting, produce cashed checks or even better, get a letter from your landlord stating that you always pay your rent on time.

- Get statements from any other person or company to whom to pay regularly and on time.

You can then present all these to a mortgage lender. No, the lender is not going to be as pleased as if you had a full credit history showing credits cards and loans and so forth. However, you have demonstrated the ability to repay debt on time, and depending on other factors (the amount of the down payment, the size of the mortgage, the credit report which shows no bad debt), you could get the real estate financing you need.

47. What If I'm Heavily in Debt?

The Quick Answer

It will make it more difficult, but usually not impossible to get a new mortgage. The amount of outstanding long-term debt you owe will influence the amount of new debt (mortgage) that you can acquire. There is, in fact, almost a direct relationship—for every dollar in long-term monthly payments you owe, subtract a dollar from the amount of income you have available to qualify for a new mortgage.

The Expanded Answer

When you apply for a mortgage, the lender will want to know your income, because that will be used to help determine the size of monthly payments you can afford. Generally speaking, the monthly payments on a mortgage where you put 20 percent down must not exceed around 31 percent of your gross income (before taxes). That drops to 28 percent for a 10 percent down deal. All of which is to say that in order to qualify, you probably will need every bit of income you can garner.

However, any long-term debt is subtracted from income available to pay for a mortgage. (It's important to differentiate between long- and short-term debt. *Short term* is any debt you can pay off in a few months. *Long term* is debt that you owe with terms lasting six months or longer. Short-term debt will not figure directly into the income/payment ratio, but it will be used when calculating your monthly living expenses.)

If you have a lot of long-term debt such as credit card payments, car loan, and so on, you may want to do what you can to reduce the amount before applying for a mortgage. The general rule is you should begin clearing up excessive debt at least six months before applying for a mortgage, but doing it anytime is a good policy.

Pay off what you can with any extra cash you have available. But keep in reserve enough cash to pay for the down payment and closing costs—normally these cannot be borrowed.

Also, work at consolidating debt. What you are looking for is a smaller payment. Often a single, large bank loan will result in cutting your total monthly payments for credit card, appliances, TV, and car loans by a significant amount. Just be sure to arrange for any consolidation loans long before you apply for a mortgage, or else it will look to the lender like you're borrowing too much, too often.

Another alternative is to sell items on which you owe money, but can live without. Good examples include boats, an extra car or motorcycle, or sports equipment. Yes, you may love these items, but if you want to qualify for a home mortgage and are close, but not quite there, on the income requirements, you may have to do without for a while.

48. What Can I Do about Some Late Payments?

The Quick Answer

Send a letter of explanation. Late payments will hurt and could keep you from getting the best (lowest-interest-rate) mortgages. Of course, the best solution is to have paid on time. But, if you didn't (or couldn't), try sending a letter to the lender explaining any extenuating circumstances that might have kept you from paying on time, emphasizing that these circumstances (hopefully) no longer exist and now your payments are prompt.

The Expanded Answer

The real problem here is that late payments suggest you are bad at managing your money. The bills come in, and instead of paying them you let them age until they are overdue. Or you spend too much one month and don't have enough cash to pay your debt, so you rob Peter to pay Paul.

What are you going to do when your debt includes a big mortgage? Lenders worry about such things.

Lenders look at late payments from three different perspectives:

How *frequent* are you late paying?

How *old* are the late payments?

How *severe* are they?

If you are always paying late, it proves you are a bad money manager and this may disqualify you from the best (conforming) mortgages. On the other hand, if you had an episode of late payments three years ago when you were ill and could not work, and have since become current on everything, a letter explaining the illness may make the problem go away. On the other hand, if your late payments were more than 120 days late and went to collections, it's a strong mark against you.

If you are, in fact, a bad money manager, it can help to admit it. Many junior colleges and adult education schools offer classes in money management (also called *home finance*). Enroll in one of these courses long before you apply for a mortgage. Then, send the lender a letter noting your deficiency in money management skills and point out you've taken a course or courses to correct the problem. Include a copy of your grade report from the course. If you can demonstrate on-time payments since you took the course, the lender may overlook earlier bad payments.

Earlier I suggested sending in a letter if late payments were caused by illness. But there could be other reasons, a layoff from a big manufacturer in the area, a flood which destroyed the office building in which you worked, anything reasonable (and true) to explain your late payments.

Of course, if you're simply a deadbeat who always pays late, don't expect a mortgage lender to be anxious to loan you $100,000 or more. If you can't demonstrate your ability to pay back what you owed on time, few people will lend you more money. You yourself would be unwise to lend money to such a person.

49. What If I Had a Repossession or a Bankruptcy?

The Quick Answer

It's a real problem. A repossession is a case of late payments carried to an extreme; bankruptcy is total financial meltdown. Either one is not likely to make a favorable impression on a lender. If either happened recently, it will probably prevent you from getting an institutional mortgage. (But you can get other types of real estate financing; see question 41.) Your only answer may be a very appealing and creative letter explaining why it happened and why it won't happen again in the future.

The Expanded Answer

The trouble with repossession is that at best it suggests very poor money management, at worst a very serious financial problem which may not be otherwise evident. Bankruptcy can be an actual threat to a lender. (Bankruptcy proceedings can sometimes prevent the lender from moving forward with a timely foreclosure and thereby recouping losses.)

Time is what you should be very careful to check out here. If it's been a long time since either repossession or bankruptcy occurred, then you have a chance of getting a mortgage. If they happened within the last two years, you can almost scratch an institutional mortgage (from a bank or savings and loan) good-bye.

Usually, at least three to five years with unblemished credit after a repossession or bankruptcy is necessary to "get your foot in the door" when applying for a mortgage. You may have to shop around, but particularly if the market for borrowers is cool, you probably can find an institutional lender (bank or savings and loan) to give you a mortgage.

If it's been 7 to 10 years since the problem, with unblemished credit since then, your chances are good to excellent of getting a mortgage. And if it's been more than 10 years, the credit-reporting agencies may not pick up the problem and the lender may simply not know!

50. What If I Recently Defaulted on a Mortgage and Went Through Foreclosure?

The Quick Answer

Find a seller who will help finance your purchase by taking back paper or look for a home with an existing *assumable* mortgage. As long as an institutional lender is aware of a recent foreclosure, the chances are slim to zero it will grant you a new mortgage. Try an equity lender (see question 41).

The Expanded Answer

It's been said often enough to be true that lenders, like elephants, have the longest memories. And foreclosure is very close to home for them. Mortgage lenders may forget or overlook an instance where you stiffed a loan company on a car loan. They may forgive late payments to a utility company. But lose a house through foreclosure and it's like a dog biting their hand. They don't tend to forget.

The reasoning seems to be that if you were willing to stop making payments and went to foreclosure in the past, you could do the same thing again in the future. No mortgage lender wants that. (Lenders are in business to make loans. When they must foreclose and take back a property, it moves the mortgage from the asset side of their books to the liability side. There's been many a lender forced out of business by making too many bad mortgages.)

Does that mean that if you ever go through foreclosure, you can never get an institutional mortgage again? Not necessarily. As noted earlier, time is a great healer. If it happened 10 years ago, and you've had great credit since then, the lender may consider you. If it happened more than 10 years ago, the lender may not know. (However, all mortgage applications require you to state whether you've ever had a foreclosure. Lying on the form can be a federal offense!)

What about that letter of explanation?

Explain away a mortgage foreclosure? Yes, sometimes. In 1996 there were terrible floods in various parts of the country. People were evacuated from their homes, some of which were damaged beyond repair. These same people often found that their employer's site was also damaged, and thus, they could not work. As a result, they had no home and no income and lost their houses to foreclosure.

Will a lender listen to such an explanation? Indeed it will. If matters were truly beyond your control by an "Act of God," most lenders will give you a shot at a new mortgage, even if the foreclosure happened only a year or so earlier. After all, you could be a very good borrower who just happened to get into hard times. Just be sure to fill your letter with ample documentation to prove what you say happened the way it did.

51. Can I Start a Totally New, Pure Credit File?

The Quick Answer

No.

The Expanded Answer

The promise of avoiding past bad credit by beginning a new credit file has been promoted by a variety of people across the country. It's an appealing concept. Your credit file at a credit-reporting agency has reports of late payments, repossessions, bankruptcy, foreclosure, and goodness only knows what else. It's the credit report from hell and there isn't a chance it will ever help you get a mortgage. So wipe it all under the table and start off fresh with a new report.

It doesn't work that way. Your credit report is tied to your social security number, name, address, and other identifying features. For you to start a new report would probably mean changing your name, getting a new social security number, and so on. It would mean you would have to lie somewhere, probably often. While you might get away with it for a while, in the long run things would probably come out into the open, particularly if you succeeded in using a "new report" to get a mortgage and then couldn't make the payments.

A lender or credit-reporting agency which discovered a false credit report would undoubtedly turn it over to the government for criminal prosecution.

What you can do is become a cash-paying citizen and eventually turn your credit around. (See question 46 for how to establish credit when paying cash.) Remember, time heals all. A number of years of good credit can make even the worst report slowly fade away.

52. Can I Get Too Much Credit?

The Quick Answer

Yes, surprisingly, you can. Mortgage lenders are particularly wary of borrowers who have large, unused lines of credit such as cards or revolving bank loans. The general rule is to have three major credit cards, but no more, and to carry small balances on all three. That should give you the best possible credit rating.

The Expanded Answer

If you're like most people, you get offers of credit cards in the mail rather frequently. It doesn't seem to matter all that much to the credit card companies how good (or bad) your credit is. If you're in a particular category that they are aiming for (students, retired, young with children, middle-aged, or just plain warm), chances are you can get a credit card. If you have good credit, it can be for lots of money. If you have bad credit, well it might have to be a debit card or for a low credit amount. But, most often you can get it!

The trouble is that many of us are tempted to apply time and again. It is not unusual these days for a family to have half a dozen credits cards, just in case. The idea is that you don't have to borrow the money...but the account is set up and ready just in case you need it.

Generally speaking this is good, logical thinking. The last time you want to approach a lender is when you desperately need money. They don't like desperate people.

Thus, setting up what amounts to lines of credit makes good sense.

However, when it comes time to borrow on a mortgage, these lines of credit can be troublesome to the mortgage lender. Part of the qualifying process involves determining your income and expenses, your ability to repay. If you have lots of unused credit, your income will appear high, your expenses low. But with credit cards, that can turn around in a moment. The day after you get the mortgage, you can go out and charge to the hilt on all of the cards. (Not really, because if you do so, it could trigger a credit agency alert, which would inform lenders of your actions so they could "pull in their horns.") At least you can charge a significant amount and incur big expenses and big payments. In short, you could turn yourself around from solvent to insolvent overnight. You might acquire payments too big for you to handle, and the ultimate result could be default on the mortgage.

That's why while mortgage lenders want you to have some credit, to show proper money management and the ability to borrow, they worry about too much credit. More than three open "trade lines" credit cards or bank lines of credit, and you might find you have trouble getting a mortgage.

The solution is to consider keeping your oldest three credit cards (mortgage lenders also look to see how long you've had a line of credit) and dump the rest. That should keep you covered, as far as a credit emergency, yet not worry a mortgage lender.

53. Should I Be Concerned about Applying Too Often for Credit?

The Quick Answer

Yes. Lenders keep track not only of how much credit you have, but how often you apply for credit. If you apply too often (more than three times in three months), they may begin to suspect you're on a borrowing spree and, if you're otherwise marginal, that can cause your mortgage to be rejected.

The Expanded Answer

I once went with my son while he shopped for a car. We must have stopped at four dealerships; at each one he made an offer and gave some credit information, but eventually did not buy. Finally, at the fifth dealership he found the deal he wanted. But by then, he was told, he didn't have good enough credit. When that fifth dealer sought a credit check, the credit agency reported my son had made four applications for credit within a short period of time.

Of course, this story has a happy ending. My son explained he had applied for credit to buy only the one car, and the dealer, who was anxious to sell, persuaded the bank to overlook the problem. However, that doesn't always happen with real estate mortgages.

Here too many applications for credit can be another nail in the coffin that buries your chances for getting a mortgage. No, it's unlikely that by itself many inquiries will do you in. But, combined with other credit problems, it might be just enough.

The answer, of course, is to be judicious in your credit applications. Only apply for what you immediately need. Be careful about accepting credit card offers that come in the mail. Each time you do, the credit card company probably checks out your credit. Apply for three credit cards in a month, and it could keep you from getting a mortgage you desperately need!

6

What Is the Right Price to Offer?

54. Should I Ask the Agent How Much to Offer?

The Quick Answer

Your agent can advise you. The question is, will it be good advice? If you're working with a seller's agent, both legally and ethically the agent should encourage you to offer full price; not very helpful. If you're working with a buyer's agent, the agent has a responsibility to provide you with good market information to help you make a decision. However, even the buyer's agent usually doesn't get paid unless and until there's a deal, so his or her interests (a quick sale) aren't really the same as yours (a good price). In short, ask the agent, but take the answer with a grain of salt.

The Expanded Answer

The truth is that the agent really doesn't know what price you should offer any more than you do. Nobody really knows what the sellers will accept once an offer is placed in front of them. I've seen hard-nosed sellers fold and meekly accept a terrible offer (for them). On the other hand, I've seen very desperate sellers, who were faced with foreclosure, hold out beyond reason for a price they believed they should get. Nobody knows for sure what a seller will do. That's why the only way to find out is to make an offer.

Your agent can be helpful in providing you with market data, which can be useful in persuading a seller to accept your offer. This frequently includes a list of what similar properties have sold for over the past year. The idea here is that if a house just like the one you want to buy sold for $200,000 last month, the one you're buying should be worth about the same.

The trouble is that if the sellers happen to be asking only $195,000, they will love your argument. On the other hand, if they're asking $250,000, they won't want to hear it.

In addition, markets are always in a state of flux. Conditions change, sometimes swiftly. I can recall back in 1989 when I was selling a home in southern California and the market suddenly dropped; values almost overnight were 10 to 20 percent less than recent sales would indicate. Smart buyers balked at paying old prices when the market was falling.

On the other hand, I was selling a home in northern California in 1997 when prices suddenly skyrocketed. Again, no one cared what the old price was. Buyers just wanted to lock in a sale at any price before the house became more expensive.

Yes, ask your agent about previous sales. But also ask about how the market is doing, and don't rely just on the agent's observations. Check with the local newspaper, which invariably will carry articles lamenting a down market or promoting an upward one. Then act accordingly.

55. Should I Hire an Appraiser?

The Quick Answer

You can, but it will be costly and the results may be of dubious value. Appraisers have a variety of methods to determine value—for income property, they look at rents; for new construction, they look at costs. But for existing residential real estate, they almost always look at recent sales of comparable properties, the same thing you can do. Sometimes having an "official appraisal" can help convince a seller to take a lower price. On the other hand, who's to say that the appraiser you hire won't come in with a price higher than you want to pay?

The Expanded Answer

Most residential appraisers work for lenders. They are called out to determine if the property is worth enough to justify the mortgage that the buyer wants. As noted above, they consider comparable properties in making their decision.

However, it's important to understand that there is no one official price for a property. Sometimes lenders will hint that they want to make the loan, so perhaps the appraiser stretches a little bit to come up with a higher price. Or perhaps a lender suggests that the government is scrutinizing new loans very carefully, so the appraiser is more conservative.

And what about market trends? What if prices just took a jump (or fell) and there aren't any recent comparables to confirm this? The appraiser can only make a good guess, the same as you.

A few years ago I accompanied an appraiser to an area of custom homes (each one was different). There were no real comparables, and prices were going up. So the appraiser took his best shot. When he expressed a value of $175,000, I told him I thought he was $100,000 too low. He just laughed. But the property sold for $260,000 with the seller carrying the financing, so no institutional loan was necessary. Armed with that comparable, the next time the appraiser went out in the area (for a home with about the same square feet), he came in at $270,000. He was just doing it by the book, while I was guesstimating by the seat of my pants. But, I happened to be right.

The upshot is that I personally don't think appraisers are necessary or even useful when trying to come up with an offering price on single-family residential real estate. (It's quite different for commercial, multiple-family, or industrial property.) But, if you want to use one, be sure you get one that's good. Appraisers who offer the American Institute of Real Estate Appraisers (MAI) or Society of Real Estate Appraisers (SREA) designation have usually been well-trained.

56. Should I Offer a Certain Percentage Less Than the Asking Price?

The Quick Answer

Certainly, in all but a hot market. The real question is, what percentage less? It's important not to employ a mechanical approach to price. You should never say, "Buyers always offer 5 percent lower than the seller's asking price, so I will, too!" Maybe 5 percent is too little, maybe it's too much. A lot depends on your reading of the seller, the market conditions, and how close to a realistic price the seller is already asking.

The Expanded Answer

Whenever I do an interview on the radio, this is the one question that I am asked more than any other. Unfortunately, I don't have a pat answer. I've heard real estate agents say, for example, "In this market, buyers are generally offering 3 percent lower than the seller's asking price."

Really, every buyer? I find that extraordinarily hard to believe. Chances are no one buyer knows any other, so how would they know how much less to offer? I don't think statistics are kept.

But they are kept on the average difference between *asking price* and *selling price* (not initial offering price) in a given area. Most agents can provide this information, and it can be a useful guide to aid you in determining if the market is hot (sellers getting full price or close to it), cold (sellers getting far below asking price), or somewhere in between.

Once again, it's important to understand that determining the correct asking price is a judgment call. And since it's your money, you have to make it.

57. When Should I Make a Lowball Offer?

The Quick Answer

A *lowball offer* is a price way below what the seller is asking, sometimes as much as 20 percent or more below. You should make this kind of offer in a cold market, where properties aren't selling, or any time you think a seller is desperate to dump the property and will grasp at any offer. Be wary, however, of making lowball offers in hot markets. Another buyer could come in with a higher offer and beat you out.

The Expanded Answer

Making a lowball offer is akin to playing poker. A good poker player doesn't just play the cards. He or she also plays the other players. To get a lowball offer accepted, you usually have to understand the seller.

In the trade this is called *motivation*. How motivated is the seller to get rid of the property? That's what you really need to find out. A highly motivated seller is ready to deal, and may accept a very low offer, even something out of left field that is totally screwy. On the other hand, a not very motivated seller may not even bother to counter a lowball offer, making it very difficult for you to continue negotiations.

Savvy buyers always try to personally meet the sellers. This is usually done while touring the property. I've known sneaky buyers who've gone back three and four times, ostensibly to see the house again, but in reality just to chat some more with the sellers. Have the sellers recently been transferred? How long has the house been on the market? Are the sellers facing some sort of pressure to sell, such as a pending foreclosure? Is there a divorce and must the house be sold before a financial resolution can be reached? Or are the sellers content to simply sit on the house for a long time, perhaps a year or more? Does the seller think he or she has made a mistake and does the seller really want to take the house off the market to live in it or to rent it out? Knowing the answer to these and similar questions goes a long way toward helping with the decision to make a lowball offer. Of course, sellers often won't say or will try to conceal their real motivation. That's why clever buyers keep going back. They keep trying to find out. And, in truth, most sellers eventually do spill the beans and tell their true motivation.

Have these investigative buyers done something illegal or even immoral? I don't think so. All buyers need information in order to make a favorable (to them) offer.

They're just doing their job. After all, consider that at the same time as the buyers are sounding out the sellers, clever sellers are sounding out the buyers! It works both ways, and the results often depend on who's the better card player (as in poker).

Of course, if you can't personally meet the sellers (they aren't home or don't live in the house), you can always call them. There's nothing to say you can't. Or you can ask the agents, who may provide useful information. (Or not—remember, a seller's agent isn't supposed to tell you, the buyer, the motivation of the seller.)

Some buyers I've seen always make a lowball initial offer, no matter what. They just want to see what the seller will do. (As noted, however, in a hot market that could allow another buyer to sneak in with a more reasonable offer and snatch up the property.)

If the seller doesn't bite, then these buyers come back with a much more reasonable offer. They come back, even if the seller doesn't counter. It's sort of like testing the waters before they jump in. Something you, too, may want to consider.

58. How Do I Know the True Market Value of the Home?

The Quick Answer

The *true market value* is what a buyer who is not under duress will pay in an arm's-length deal with full disclosure about all of the attributes and drawbacks of the property. If you know everything about the home, both good and bad, and aren't pressured to buy because of time or other constraints (such as you've moving to a new area and must find a house this weekend!), then what you pay determines the true market value.

The Expanded Answer

The real question that bothers many buyers is, "Am I leaving anything on the table? Could I have gotten a better price if I had been more insistent, more daring?"

In the old days it was very hard to know the answer to this question. Buyer and seller negotiated, and a deal was struck. Who knew how much more the other side might have conceded?

Today, however, it's not as hard to find out. The reason is that when buying a home, a deal is no longer a deal when it's made. It's a deal weeks later when the buyers have approved all the inspections and disclosures the sellers have offered. During that time, additional negotiations can take place.

Recently a friend was buying a home, and she negotiated a price. However, she was concerned that the sellers would have taken less than she offered. When the inspection came back, it indicated the roof was in poor shape, but serviceable. So she insisted that the sellers put on a new roof. At first the sellers balked, but then agreed to split the cost, some $4000. My friend had this written into the contract in the form that the "seller would provide $4000 in nonrecurring closing costs to the buyer." This meant that the price was just knocked down by $4000 (*nonrecurring* meant that it wouldn't influence the loan from the lender and that the buyer could use the money to help pay those closing costs which don't recur, such as title insurance, escrow charges, points, and so on. Then she let the roof go; she had just saved $4000 on the deal.

This type of "after deal" negotiating takes place regularly today. It's a way of refining the determination of true market value, a way for buyers to feel more confident that they are paying the right price for the home they are buying.

59. Should I Offer My Top Price?

The Quick Answer

The implication, of course, is that you have a top price. I believe that it's a real mistake to set a top price when buying real estate. The reason is that at least half the deal is terms. What if the seller wants more than you're prepared to pay, but offers you such favorable terms that it's a better deal for you? Setting a top price could keep you from making this deal. Be flexible. Remember, buying real estate is always a combination of price *and* terms. Sometimes you may actually want to offer far more than your "top" price, to get the better terms!

The Expanded Answer

If we all bought for cash, then price would be everything and we could set a top limit. But the truth is very few people pay cash for homes. Almost everything is financed. And therein lie all kinds of opportunities.

For example, let's say that you want to buy a home, and you don't want to pay more than $125,000. But the seller wants $130,000 and won't budge.

You aren't paying cash; you're getting a mortgage. So, instead of getting a new first mortgage for the entire amount, ask the seller to carry back a second mortgage for 20 percent of the sales price (you'll put 20 percent down and you'll get a new first mortgage for 60 percent). Yes, you'll pay what the seller is asking, $130,000. But you want the seller to carry the second mortgage at an interest rate of 4 percent.

Now, is that a good deal for you? Chances are the new first mortgage will carry an interest rate of close to 8 percent, depending on the market at the time. Your second will be for half that amount. Think of the interest you'll be saving. On a $20,000 mortgage, that's $800 a year. In 7 years (statistically about as long as you'll keep the house), it will be $5600. It's almost the same as paying $5000 less for the property!

Is it a good deal for the sellers? Could be, if they are hung up on getting their price. I've seen many sellers accept onerous terms, just so they could say they didn't budge below a certain amount. No, you didn't get your price; but you did get the house, and the terms you got offset the extra amount you paid. It's definitely a win-win situation.

The moral of this story is to be very careful when talking about top-price offers. You should never determine in advance what your top price is. Just get a feel for what the market value of the house is and what you can afford to come up with in terms of the down payment and monthly payments, then see if a deal to satisfy all can be negotiated.

60. Should I Ever Offer More Than the Asking Price?

The Quick Answer

Yes, you may have to. In a hot market with few properties for sale (or a very low-priced property) and lots of buyers competing, you may need to offer more than the asking price to get the deal! No, this doesn't happen often, but sometimes there are multiple offers on the same property. If you want the home and are competing with two, three, or more other buyers, usually it's the highest offer that wins.

The Expanded Answer

Offering more than asking price is rarely done, but sometimes it is the only strategy that wins. I have been involved in purchases where, for example, for whatever reason the seller priced the property well below what I considered market value. Of course, I was not the only one to realize this. Other buyers saw the opportunity as well, and within hours of the house coming onto the market, there were many offers.

Usually you will know when you are in a competition. It will be obvious that many other people also want the property. Typically, you or your agent will call the selling agent (or the sellers directly if no agent is involved), and you will be told that many people are looking at the property and several offers are imminent (or may have already been received). If you really want the property, speed now is of the essence and the question of how much to offer becomes critical.

In such a situation, many buyers will simply offer full price. If the sellers are asking $105,000, simply give them what they want. That would work, if you were the only buyer. However, in real estate, offers are presented as they are received. (At least that's the way it's supposed to be done!) That means that just because your offer is first, doesn't mean it will keep other offers away. If another offer comes in while the sellers are deliberating over yours, that second offer will be given to them immediately. It will interrupt their deliberations. It won't be held aside until they make their decision on your offer.

In order to be the winning offer, yours must now be higher (or better) than the others. (In a situation such as this, many offers come in for *cash,* meaning the buyer will pay cash down to a new first loan. Thus, offering better terms instead of a higher price can be difficult if not impossible.)

What you must do is determine how much the home is worth to you. If it's underpriced, how much higher than the asking price can you go and still justify the purchase? If its a hot market with prices rapidly appreciating, how much appreciation are you willing to gamble on?

I have been involved in competitive-offer situations. In one situation, the winning buyers offered 5 percent over the asking price and later regretted it, because they paid too much. In another situation, the buyers offered 7 percent over asking and were thrilled to get what they perceived as still a bargain.

This is a judgment call, where you must calculate what price you can live with and then act swiftly.

61. How Big a Deposit Should I Give?

The Quick Answer

The purpose of the deposit is to assure the seller that you are serious in your offer. That's why it is sometimes called *earnest money*. Once the money is put up, it's at risk to you. If you back out of the deal, you stand to lose the deposit. Therefore, you want to offer enough to satisfy the seller that you are serious, yet not offer so much you could suffer a serious financial loss if the deal doesn't go through. Generally speaking I have found the following deposit schedule helpful:

Property Value	Deposit
Under $100,000	$2500
$100,000 to $350,000	$5000–$7500
$350,000 to $500,000	$7500 to $10,000
Over $500,000	$10,000 to $15,000 or more

The Expanded Answer

The more you put up as a deposit, the more serious the seller is likely to think you are. However, some buyers feel they can make up for a weak offer with a big deposit. They hope to impress the sellers with a large amount of cash.

These days, however, sellers are rarely so impressed. The truth is that the deposit money is not at as much risk as it used to be. In most states you, as a buyer, often have weeks to conduct inspections and approve disclosures. During this time you can usually back out of the deal with no loss of deposit.

Even after having signed off on all reports and disclosures, savvy buyers often leave contingencies (discussed in Chapter 7) that offer them a back door out without penalty. In some cases, the only way the seller can eventually get your money is to go to court and sue for it—not something most sellers will do while they are trying to sell their home. (Many contracts now offer a "liquidated damages" clause that makes it easier for the seller to claim your deposit, but harder to sue you.)

That doesn't mean you can't lose your deposit if you back out of the deal—you can. It's just that savvy sellers know it's not a slam dunk for them to get it and, hence, are not so impressed with it.

My own suggestion is that you put up between $5000 and $10,000 depending on the size of the deal. Most sellers accept that this is enough to hold the property for the month or so it takes to close and are okay with it. If the deposit is an issue with the sellers, they will usually come back asking you to increase the amount, usually after all the disclosure and inspection contingencies have been removed. If you still want the property, you can increase your deposit at that time.

7

What Should I Insist Go into the Sales Agreement?

62. Should I Consult an Attorney Before I Sign?

The Quick Answer

The safe answer is, "Yes," always. However, in most of the country and especially on the West Coast, buyers almost never consult attorneys before signing a purchase agreement. Indeed, while on the East Coast real estate attorneys are readily available, on the West Coast it's hard to find one. In practice, the vast majority of purchases conducted by agents and signed without benefit of an attorney go perfectly well. However, if something should go wrong, then you could rue the day you didn't first seek competent counsel.

The Expanded Answer

A purchase agreement is intended to be a legally binding contract. When I first became involved in real estate over 30 years ago, it was a single-page document with a few paragraphs of standardized text and the majority of items written in by hand.

Today it's typically 5 to 10 pages long, consisting almost entirely of paragraphs crafted by attorneys. About the only thing left to fill in is the address, the price, the deposit, and the loan amount.

The reason for the metamorphosis in sales agreements is that over the years litigation between buyers, sellers, and agents has demonstrated that the old contracts were loose and easily broken. Today's contracts are designed to be tighter and more difficult for either buyer or seller to break. The way this is accomplished by agents (who for the most part are not attorneys) is to try to foresee all the potential problems and then have a lawyer construct the appropriate language in a prewritten contract. In essence, almost everything in a modern contract is *boilerplate*, standardized legally vetted paragraphs.

However, purchase agreements cannot foresee all possible problems. Often contingencies must be written in, and sometimes the situation of the buyer, seller, or the property is unusual. Only you, or your attorney, can protect your interests here.

Be wary, however, of attorneys who seem to go out of their way to earn their fee by adding complicated clauses that give you excessive protection. In their zeal to protect you, the attorney may create an offer that is so one-sided, the sellers won't accept. It's an old joke in real estate that when you bring in the attorneys, you throw out the deal!

Many buyers (probably a significant majority) who have purchased real estate in the past did not use attorneys and quite successfully completed transactions. On the other hand, if this is your first time out, or there is anything unusual about the transaction or anything you are concerned about, you probably will want to get a lawyer to look things over for you, just to be sure. (Attorney's fees here are usually quite low—$500 to $1000 to handle the entire transaction!)

Also, remember that, as noted, the vast majority of real estate agents are not attorneys. Indeed, when asked to give legal advice, they will almost universally respond that they are not qualified and will not do so. Nevertheless, I have known many agents whose practical knowledge of real estate law far exceeds that of many attorneys I have known!

63. Should I Insist on Having a Contingency, or an "Escape," Clause Inserted?

The Quick Answer

Yes...and no. A *contingency clause* makes the purchase subject to certain conditions being met. (That's why it's also sometimes referred to as a *subject-to clause*.) A common example is a clause inserted into the sales agreement which states that the sale is subject to the buyers getting a new mortgage at a particular interest rate and payment. If the buyers don't get a new mortgage, there's no sale. Buyers like to include contingency clauses because it gives them a graceful way to back out of the deal without losing their deposit, if things don't work out the way they want. Sellers, however, may refuse to accept contracts with contingency clauses that give buyers too much wiggle room. If you insist on such a clause, it could protect you, but it also might cost you the deal.

The Expanded Answer

Often a contingency clause is vitally necessary for your protection. For example, you are buying a home and plan to use the money from the sale of your current home to pay for the new one. Only the deal hasn't closed on your old home, and you can't be sure it will. Therefore, you may want to insert a clause which states that the purchase of the new home is contingent upon the sale of the old. It's perfectly reasonable, to you.

However, from the sellers' perspective, to sign a sales agreement with such a clause in it might be foolish. The sellers would be tying up the sale of their home in the hope your old house would sell. Now, instead of worrying about selling just one house, the sellers have to worry about the sale of two! Further, if for any reason your old home doesn't sell, their deal doesn't go through either. Therefore, such a clause, though probably necessary for you as a buyer in such a situation, can be a deal wrecker from the sellers' perspective. Only if the market is very weak, the sellers are grasping for straws, or your house is already sold and in escrow are they likely to go for it.

However, you can make any contingency more enticing by limiting it, usually in terms of time. You could say that the sale is subject to your escrow (on your old house) closing within two weeks. If it doesn't close by then, the deal's off. Here the sellers are only tying up their property for a short time. Further, during that time you would normally be inspecting their property and going through disclosures—it's little time wasted. Further, you can agree to let the sellers continue to show the property and to accept "backup offers" during the two weeks. Now you have constructed a far more acceptable offer, from the sellers' perspective.

But note, each step above weakens your position. Instead of tying up the sellers' home, you've only locked it in for two weeks. If your house doesn't sell by then, you're back to ground zero. (Almost...after a couple of weeks, if it looks like the sale of your old home will only take a few more days, most sellers will go along.)

You can insert anything as a contingency in a sales agreement, even ridiculous things. For example, you could make the sale contingent upon the melting of the polar ice caps or the approval of the home by your Uncle Harry in Australia. Just remember, however, that the more unlimited and wild the contingency, the less likely the seller is to accept it.

Most good agents and attorneys can draft a proper contingency clause for you.

64. When Should I Demand Occupancy?

The Quick Answer

Normally, occupancy is given at the close of escrow, when the sale is consummated. The date of occupancy is one of the most important considerations in a sales agreement. You want to be sure it's in the contract. While the close of escrow is common, occupancy can be given anytime, before or later. Sometimes you want a date a long way off, because your kids are in school and you want to wait until school ends before moving. Other times you may have a reason to move sooner. In situations such as these, the date of occupancy can be a deal point. Be sure it's negotiated up front, or else you may not get a choice later on.

The Expanded Answer

Since there are good reasons for giving occupancy on the day escrow closes, you may want to insist on a long or short escrow. For example, if you don't want (or need) to occupy the property for two months, insist on a 60-day escrow. That way you won't get the property sooner than needed, and you won't have to pay the mortgage, taxes, and other ongoing costs during that time.

On the other hand, perhaps the property is vacant and you need to move in within two weeks. You can demand that escrow close within two weeks and occupancy be given then. Just keep in mind, however, that it usually takes upwards of a month for you to get financing, and it may be impossible to close escrow and consummate the deal so quickly. Don't ask for the impossible.

You can ask for occupancy before escrow closes. This, however, would be a big concession and risk for the sellers. The reason is that if you move in while they still own the property, you become, in effect, a tenant. If the deal should not close for any reason, you could stay there until they were forced to evict you.

As a seller, I have allowed buyers to move in prior to the close of escrow. But, I had them sign a strict rental agreement and pay rent up front, including a hefty security deposit large enough to cover my costs if eviction became necessary. In my case, the deal went through, and the buyers got back all but a few weeks of rent money.

As a buyer, you may need to propose such a deal to a seller. If all the other terms and the price are acceptable, a seller may go along. Just remember, however, making such a demand weakens your offer. Most sellers don't want the hassle involved and would rather accept a clean deal with occupancy given when the sale is closed.

65. Should I Agree to a Liquidated Damages Clause and an Arbitration Clause?

The Quick Answer

Most current real estate contracts contain both of these clauses. A *liquidated damages clause* usually says that if both you and the seller agree to the sale, and you later back out of the deal without justification, you lose your deposit...the seller, however, can't sue you to complete the transaction. An *arbitration clause* usually says that in the event of a dispute, you agree to binding arbitration between you, the agent(s), and/or the sellers. Be aware that when you sign these clauses, you may be giving up some of your rights, particularly to seek litigation as a recourse. On the other hand, you could also be avoiding a lot of potential hassle later on if something goes wrong. This is one of those areas you would want your attorney to advise you on.

The Expanded Answer

There are definitely two camps on this one. On one side tend to be real estate agents who want to avoid lawsuits. Often they have been involved in them in the past. The agents know that these lawsuits can be time-consuming, extremely expensive, and bad for business and that they may ultimately produce mixed results.

On the other side are attorneys who sometimes point out that being able to sue the other party is an important and valuable right. You might be damaged by the sellers' actions. For example, you have a signed purchase agreement with a seller, and based on that you make a job decision—you leave your old distant employer and accept work with a new local employer. The deal seems fine until the final days when the seller decides for reasons unfathomable to you (sometimes because a far bigger offer has come in, other times because of a change in family plans, or for yet other reasons) not to sell. The seller simply refuses to sign the deed and conclude the sale.

Now your anticipated home at your new job doesn't exist. Housing is tight, and you have to rent a motel. The hassle causes you trouble at work, and you're fired. Now you have no house and no job. Do you want to sue the seller? You bet you do! An attorney might point out that you have a good case. However, you signed an arbitration clause!

In short, there are good reasons to sign and not to sign the liquidated damages and the arbitration clauses. (Never mind that the agent encourages you to sign because it might happen to make things easier for the broker—that's not your concern.) Further, each person's position is different.

That's why you need some good *practical* legal advice here. A practicing real estate attorney can often set out the consequences in your particular case in just a few minutes. That can make the decision far easier.

66. Should I Demand a Final Walk-Through Inspection?

The Quick Answer

Yes. The purpose of having a final walk-through inspection, usually conducted a day or two before the close of escrow (when the sale is completed) and before you sign your final papers, is to give you the opportunity to be sure the property is as it was when you first saw it. By now the sellers have moved, and you can see that they have left behind the floor and wall coverings (assuming they were part of the deal) and have left the place in relatively good condition. If there is anything missing or damaged, now is the time to complain—before the deal closes and while you still have leverage. A provision for a final inspection must be inserted into the sales agreement for you to have one. Most agents and attorneys can easily handle this.

The Expanded Answer

In the old days too often buyers would take possession only to find that the sellers had walked off with window coverings, rugs, even appliances that appeared to be built in! Today, most contracts include a paragraph that states that wall and window coverings, wall-to-wall carpets, and all built-ins are part of the deal and are to remain. To be sure there are no surprises, a walk-through inspection just prior to closing is a good idea.

Additionally, between the time the sellers signed the sales agreement and the close of escrow, you also want to be sure the sellers haven't thrown any wild parties that damaged the carpeting, the walls, or anything else. Again, the final walk-through inspection covers this.

Finally, there is the matter of cleanliness. This, like beauty, is in the eye of the beholder. You may find that when furniture is moved away from walls, scratches and dirt marks show up. Furniture may also conceal marks on carpeting. And the place may not be up to your standards of cleanliness. Unfortunately, unless it is far dirtier than when you first saw it, or there are serious problems with the carpeting or actual holes in the walls, there isn't a great deal you can do about this. The sellers can claim, and with a great deal of justification, that this is the way it always was. You just never looked closely enough. In other words, plan on doing some cleaning when you move in.

A word of caution if the former occupants had pets. Be sure the carpet or flooring does not contain urine. The smell is virtually impossible to remove and could require replacement of carpeting, padding, and even the flooring underneath!

Items to watch for during the final inspection include:

Appliances.   Are they all there; do they all work?

Wall coverings, etc.   Are the wall coverings, shades, blinds, curtains, etc., as specified in the contract?

Carpeting.   Check for urine stains and smells in the wall-to-wall carpeting; however, unless specified in the contract, throw rugs usually do *not* go with the house.

Heater/air conditioner.   Do they work?

General cleanliness.   It should be reasonably clean, but don't expect perfection here.

Damage.   Check for holes in walls, burns or severe marks in carpeting.

Miscellaneous.   Check for anything else that's significantly different from when you first saw the property.

If there are any problems, bring them to the attention of the agent and the seller immediately. In most cases these things can be quickly cleared up. Serious problems, however, may make you decide to hold off signing until they are fixed.

However, keep in mind that by this time, contingencies have normally all been removed and you could open yourself up to legal action by the sellers if you refuse to sign. In other words, you'd better have some pretty good reasons for holding back. It is a very risky strategy to try to use the final inspection as an excuse to back out of the deal, unless some very serious problem is discovered.

67. Should I Demand an Overall Home Inspection?

The Quick Answer

Yes, you should. It should be written into the sales agreement as a contingency typically allowing you time to get the inspection (usually around 10 days) and then time to evaluate the results and determine if you want to continue on with the sale (perhaps another 5 days).

The Expanded Answer

From the buyer's perspective there are two purposes in having the home inspected. The first and most obvious is to determine if there are any hidden defects. A good home inspector will check for all sorts of problems from exposed wiring to a cracked foundation, none of which you may have discovered yourself or may have been disclosed by the sellers. Once you receive the inspector's report (assuming your approval of it was written in as a contingency), you can decide, based on it, whether or not you want to continue with the purchase.

The second purpose is to help you renegotiate the price and/or terms with the sellers after you have concluded the sales agreement. The home inspection, except in the case of very new, well-built homes, almost always uncovers something. Usually it is minor, but many times it is major. What's important to remember is that most (but not all) such problems can be solved with money.

For example, it may turn out that the roof leaks or is nearing the end of its useful life and needs to be replaced sometime soon. Are you going to replace it? It could cost upwards of $10,000.

However, you now tell the sellers that you have discovered a problem with the roof. You would like them to either put on a new roof or give you $10,000 off the price, *or* you won't buy the property.

If they want to sell, the sellers must now make some concessions. (The interesting thing about inspection reports is that the sellers are supposed to show *all* reports to any other prospective buyers, so they can't easily back out of the sale with you and then hide the roof problem from the next buyers!)

The sellers, however, may balk at the high price tag for repairs. They may offer to split the cost with you. You call up the roof inspector and ask him just how long will that roof really last? He explains it could be patched for $1000 and might last another five years.

You agree to the $5000 from the seller. You can accept this as a straight price reduction, or the sellers could offer it toward your nonrecurring closing costs (in effect paying for many of your closing costs). The latter course may prove the wiser because if you have a clause written into the contract stating the price was reduced because of a bad roof, the lender may refuse to fund a mortgage until the roof is, indeed, replaced.

The inspection report has helped you negotiate a better deal.

In addition, it's a good idea to have sellers pay for a home warranty insurance plan to insure the workability of appliances and other systems after you move in—see question 99.

68. Can I Include Any Personal Property (Refrigerator, Lamps, etc.) in the Sale?

The Quick Answer

Yes, you can. But it can screw up the deal. Normally, the transaction is for *real* property, which includes the land and anything attached to it, such as the house, garage, fences, and so forth. By simply adding a clause, you can include any personal property, even the furniture of the sellers! Any agent or attorney can draft such a clause for you. However, the lender may now balk at giving you full financing, because the loan would be covering personal property as well as real estate.

The Expanded Answer

When you include personal property, particularly items such as furniture, carpeting (throw rugs), or similar obviously personal items, you cast the value of the sale's price in doubt. For example, let's say you are buying a home for $150,000, but are including an entire house full of furniture. Does the $150,000 reflect the true price of the home, or is it an inflated price pushed higher than true market value because of the personal property included?

There could be tax consequences to you of an inflated price. It could affect your tax basis in the property as well as the amount of property tax you pay. There might even be sales tax to pay on the personal property. Check with your accountant here.

Additionally, it could affect your ability to get needed financing. All lenders look at the sales agreement. The moment the lender sees that personal property is included, particularly a lot of it, the sales price is going to be suspect. The lender may say, for example, that the true sales price was in reality only $140,000 because you got $10,000 in personal property.

The consequence of this is that the mortgage could be based on a $140,000 sales price instead of $150,000. In short, you could have to come up with $10,000 more cash!

One way around this problem is to not include personal property in the real estate sales agreement. Rather, have a separate agreement drawn up for the personal property.

69. Should I Argue over the Date of Prorations?

The Quick Answer

It may or may not be to your advantage to do so. *To prorate* means to divide and refers to items such as taxes, insurance, home owner's dues, and other items that typically run for long periods of time. When you buy, some items may have been prepaid by the seller; others may be owing. The date of proration refers to the date that the amounts are divided between both parties. Usually prorations are made the day escrow closes, but sometimes moving the date of prorations (normally spelled out in the contract) can save you a sizable amount of money.

The Expanded Answer

The best way to understand this is to take an example. Real estate taxes are usually assessed on a yearly basis, from June 30 to July 1. However, they are normally paid twice annually, often in December and March. Let's say that you buy a home with the sale to close May 1 and that the taxes on the property are $3600 a year, or $300 a month. If the sale closes on May 1 and the tax year in your area ends June 30, there will be two months' worth of taxes before the end of the tax year, or $600. Since the taxes were probably paid in full in March by the sellers (assuming they aren't delinquent), the sellers have already paid the taxes to June 30. Hence, you will owe the sellers two months' worth, or $600 in taxes.

However, if you move the date of prorations back to June 30, then you won't owe the sellers anything. That's because the division will be made at the end of the tax year. In effect, the sellers will have paid two months' worth of your taxes.

Why would a seller agree to this? Most sellers wouldn't, unless it was a deal point—a concession the sellers made for some other concession you might make. It's something to consider when structuring your offer. Also, keep in mind that you may not be able to deduct the two months' worth of taxes paid by the sellers from your income taxes; see your accountant.

70. How Should I Hold Title?

The Quick Answer

You must normally indicate in the sales agreement how you will take title. There are several ways to hold title: community property, joint tenants, tenants in common, to name a few. There are very specific legal consequences of each different type, and deciding how to hold title is an important matter. Since your situation can be radically different from some other buyer's, only your personal attorney can give you appropriate advice.

The Expanded Answer

For an overview, here are what the different types of titles mean. (Note: these sometimes go by different names in the various states.)

Community Property. This title is available only in some states; it can usually be taken only by a husband and wife who are legally married. There are very specific benefits here. If one spouse dies, the other automatically inherits the deceased's portion of the property.

Further, there can be a big tax advantage. Upon death of one spouse, the other automatically gets a "stepped-up tax basis." An example should make this clear: Let's say you have a home worth $700,000 on which your tax basis is $100,000. (You bought it originally for $100,000 years ago, and it's gone way up in value.) Were you to sell this property, you would have a capital gain of $600,000 (not taking into account such things as improvements, costs of sale, and so on) on which you would be taxed.

But, if your spouse dies, then the basis of the property immediately jumps up from $100,000 to $700,000. Now were you to sell, you would have no capital gain and no tax to pay! Check with your accountant or tax adviser for details and to determine whether this type of a title would be in your best interests.

Joint Tenancy. Here the critical factor is survival. When one joint tenant dies, his or her interest in the property passes immediately to the other joint tenant. An important consideration is that you cannot will your portion of the property to someone else.

Tenants in Common. Here you can determine who will get your interest in the property upon your death. Your interest will transfer depending on your will (if you have one) or usually upon the laws of the state in which you reside (if you don't have a will). Since state laws can often divide the property of the deceased in strange ways (some to the parents, some to the children, some to the spouse, and so on), it's a good argument for having a will.

As noted earlier, how you take title is an important legal decision and should not be taken lightly. However, the decision can be made ahead of time, not when you're in the midst of negotiating over the purchase of a home. It can be discussed at the same time you consult an attorney to have a will drawn up or to create a living trust for your children.

8

How Do I Get the Seller to Accept My Price and Terms?

71. How Much Time Should I Allow the Sellers to Consider My Offer?

The Quick Answer

Allow the sellers as short a time as is practical, often just one day. You want them to not only consider, but *act* on your offer. If you give them too long, they may get to arguing between themselves and not be able to come to an agreement. Or, worse, another better offer may come in from other buyers, and they may accept it rather than yours.

The Expanded Answer

What you want is a swift reply to your offer, presumably an acceptance or at least a counteroffer. In other words, you want to engage the sellers in immediate negotiation. If the sellers are available, many good agents will only allow them until that evening to accept. For example, if you make the offer at 1 p.m. in the afternoon, you may want to give the sellers only until 10 p.m. of that same day to accept. If the sellers are unavailable that day, you may want to allow them only 24 hours to accept, assuming they can be reached by the next day.

Some, in my opinion, poor agents will suggest that you allow the sellers "ample time to consider your offer." I've seen agents suggest three days or more. Their reasoning is that the sellers need to be able to look at your offer from all sides, perhaps consult with their attorney, their parents, the aunt in Australia.

I don't believe this is good advice. For one thing, the longer your offer is on the table, the more opportunity there is for other buyers to slip in another offer, perhaps better than yours. Remember, just because you've presented an offer that the sellers are considering does not mean they can't consider and accept a different offer from other buyers. Indeed, agents are required to present all offers to sellers as soon as they are received, not wait while the sellers consider one at a time.

Further, by giving the sellers a short time to accept, you force them to make a decision. You put them on the spot. Either they accept (or counter) now, or your offer will be withdrawn and they could lose a sale. Many a seller has agreed to less than they hoped to get for fear of losing a buyer entirely.

Finally, a short time frame often is a test of the mettle of your agent (who, presumably, presents the offer). Good agents like the leverage the short time frame gives them. They can tell the sellers, "My buyers like your property, but yours isn't the only one they are considering. If you don't agree to their offer (or make a good counter), they'll go elsewhere."

By the way, don't be coerced into giving a longer time for acceptance just because the sellers happen to not live nearby. With modern fax lines, it really doesn't matter if the sellers are next door or across the country. The offer can be faxed to them and the negotiations held over the phone. They can fax back a signed offer (or counter) immediately. The only reason for allowing more time for acceptance usually is if one or both sellers cannot be reached (they're on vacation, out of the country, and so on).

72. What If the Sellers Reject My Offer?

The Quick Answer

If the sellers do not accept your offer exactly as presented (no changes of any kind) within the time limits you've given, your offer is automatically rejected. Your commitment to the offer expires the moment the time period is up, or the sellers reject it, or you withdraw it. You can demand your deposit back and can now feel free to walk away from the property.

The Expanded Answer

It's important to remember two things here: First, you can withdraw your offer at any time up until it has been accepted by the sellers. For example, you give the sellers until 10 p.m. to accept. But at 6 p.m. you discover a house that you like a whole lot better. You want to get out of the original offer you made, so you can buy the second house. You call your agent and are told the sellers are considering your offer and probably will sign within the hour. You tell your agent that the offer is withdrawn immediately and you want your deposit back. In theory, you may withdraw your offer at any time *until you are informed* of the sellers' written acceptance.

Second, the sellers cannot both accept and modify your offer. Too often I've heard agents call their buyers and say, "Congratulations, you've bought a home! I'll be by for you to initial a couple of minor changes the sellers have made in the purchase agreement."

No way! If the sellers change anything at all, you're not committed to your offer, you haven't bought the property, there's been no deal made. The only way you're committed to your offer is if the sellers accept it as you signed it with no changes of any kind (within the time frame you've given for acceptance). The minute they make changes, it becomes a counteroffer. In other words, they've rejected your offer and are now countering with an alternative. You may feel free to accept or reject (or yourself counter) their counteroffer.

It's important to understand that this applies no matter how trivial appearing their change may be. For example, your offer may state that the deal is to close and you are to be given possession on the 25th of the month. The sellers agree to your price and terms; however, they change the offer to state that the deal is to close on the 30th, so they don't have to pay an additional 5 days interest (or rent) when they move to their new home.

It's now a counteroffer. You can simply say, "Nope," and walk away.

Of course, the date may make no difference to you and you'll be happy to accept. On the other hand, maybe now you'll think about the whole deal and decide you really don't want that property after all. (It's something the sellers have to consider seriously, before countering an offer.)

73. What If the Sellers Counter My Offer?

The Quick Answer

Now the shoe is on the other foot. In order to be assured of a deal, you must accept their counteroffer exactly as presented within the time frame they've given you. If you wait too long, if you change anything in the counter offer, they are not committed to going through with the deal they offer.

The Expanded Answer

As a practical matter, in most deals buyers and sellers counteroffer each other repeatedly, winnowing their differences away until finally a mutually acceptable compromise is agreed upon. I've seen deals where counteroffers fly back and forth until the wee hours of the morning before agreement is finally achieved. (On the other hand, sometimes it's just impossible to make that deal.) It is important to remember, however, that each time you reject a sellers' counteroffer and counter back, you're taking the chance that the sellers could simply fold up their tents and walk away.

Negotiating through counteroffers is, in truth, a kind of art form. It requires skill, patience, and no small amount of intestinal fortitude. It's akin to playing poker. You don't really know how strong the sellers' hand is, and they're not sure about your hand. You want to get them to concede as much as possible, and at the same time you want to give up as little as you have to. Some people enjoy the contest; others can't stand it.

By the way, as noted elsewhere, beware of sticking to a "top price" when negotiating. For example, some buyers believe that they will get the best deal if they establish a top price well in advance of making an offer. This is the maximum amount they will pay for the property. No matter what the sellers counter, they won't go a dime above this amount. Usually, inexperienced and fearful buyers are "top pricers." They are afraid of being tricked by agents or sellers into paying more than they want to for the property, so they establish a maximum in advance, believing it will save them.

Being hard-nosed about price can, indeed, sometimes get you a good deal. But it can just as often lose a good deal. (See also question 59.)

74. How Fast Should I Counter Back?

The Quick Answer

Fairly quickly. If you don't accept the sellers' counteroffer exactly as presented, but instead want to make changes, then it's a totally new offer from you—a counter-counteroffer, so to speak. You want to make this counter soon, usually within a day, while the sellers are still psychologically engaged in the deal.

The Expanded Answer

While it's usual to limit any offers (or counters) by a time period, once you're into countering back and forth things tend to fly fast. I've seen these counters come whizzing one right after the other, either by fax or carried by hand.

That doesn't mean you shouldn't put a limit on the time for acceptance of your counter. If you don't, then the offer is open until withdrawn (by you) and at any time the sellers might say, "Let's just pull back and wait a few days."

That's why I always suggest making any counter for as short a time as possible, often 24 hours or less. As noted earlier, this puts the sellers on the spot. They must act, which is exactly what you want them to do. (Remember, there's always a chance another offer could come in from other buyers and torpedo yours.)

It's worth noting that there are certain tactics involved in negotiating here. If you receive the sellers' counter and then immediately counter back, the sellers may think that you really haven't taken the time to seriously consider their previous counter. Or, they may feel that you are very anxious—countering so quickly. They may feel that your most recent offer isn't your best, and your quick counter may cause them to hold back from accepting it, perhaps countering you once again.

It's for this reason that I will often hold back a few hours, sometimes as much as overnight, even though I've already made my countering decision. I want the sellers to think that I'm considering their offer very carefully. I also want them to consider that perhaps I'll simply reject their latest counter and walk away, which is my privilege. In other words, I want to keep the sellers off balance. It's better if they think they've got a finicky buyer who might just as well walk away from the negotiating table as stay and continue to play the game. This encourages the sellers to take fewer chances and to make each of their counteroffers as good as possible.

75. How Do I Know When the Sellers Have Made Their Last Best Offer?

The Quick Answer

This is something you can never know for sure. Indeed, even the sellers may not know if they would have accepted less, unless and until the situation were presented to them. You can, however, get a feel for what the sellers will do by how they act. For example, once you're into countering each other, they may initially come down a substantial amount of money. However, as the negotiating progresses, their concessions may become smaller and smaller. This indicates you are probably very close to their limits.

The Expanded Answer

The trick is to keep the sellers negotiating, yet to always have your offers below what the sellers are asking (in both price and terms). It's important to understand, however, that to play this kind of hard-ball negotiating, you must be willing to lose the deal. The reason is you never know (sometimes until it's too late) when you've exceeded the sellers' tolerance and they simply stop playing.

This is particularly the case when buyers lowball sellers. For example, the sellers may originally be asking $200,000, and you lowball at $150,000 (25 percent less than the asking price). Through counteroffers the sellers have come down to $190,000, and you've come up to $160,000. You're still miles apart.

Suddenly the sellers let you know that they're not interested in any more negotiations. Either you accept their last offer (usually within a very short time limit), or forget it. In other words, take it or leave it.

Does this mean you've reached their lowest offer? Not necessarily. It may just mean that they perceive you're so far apart that there's no hope for negotiations any longer. Indeed, maybe they might be willing to accept $185,000 or even $180,000, but your offers are so far below that they simply don't feel it's worth keeping the conversation going.

When this happens you have two choices. You can simply walk away. Or you can make a serious offer. You can now, for example, come up $20,000 and offer $180,000, which might be something they would have accepted.

Only now they're suspicious. If you're interested enough to make such a serious increase in your offer, how much further might you increase it if they just hang tight?

This is the great danger of the lowball offer. If the sellers doesn't go for it, you've got no place else to go but up and may end up paying more than you would have if you had come in with a more reasonable offer initially.

There are all sorts of negotiating strategies that you can attempt. For more on these I suggest my book *Tips & Traps When Negotiating Real Estate* (McGraw-Hill, 1995).

76. When Should I Walk Away and Stop Offering to Buy?

The Quick Answer

Walking away can be a very strong negotiating ploy. It can also be a good idea if you discover that you really don't want the deal or the property. However, before you do it, be sure that you're straight in your own mind about losing the purchase. If you walk away and nobody comes running after you to bring you back to the negotiating table, you might just have to start looking for another property.

The Expanded Answer

In a way it's like negotiating for the purchase of a car. I've been in dealerships where the salespeople tell me that they've given me the best offer they can. I've talked to the salesperson, the manager, even the dealership owner. They swear to me that I'm taking away all of their profit, and they'd be selling the car at a loss to go any lower.

Okay, I've said, but I just don't want to pay that much. I've gotten up, walked out the door, and am just about to the sidewalk when the salesperson comes running up and says something to the effect that they're trying to figure some way to work things out...yes, they can make the deal, only please come back.

Something similar can happen in real estate. The sellers may send you a counter with the explicit message that this is their last, best offer. Take it or leave it, they can't go any lower.

Faced with this alternative, I usually decide whether I can live with the deal. If I can, I take it. To my mind, it probably isn't worth any more hassle if I've gotten everything I want already.

On the other hand, if the price or the terms aren't what I want, I may simply get up and walk away, not make another counter. After all, the sellers have told me, take it or leave it—I'm leaving it.

Will they (or the agent) come running after me as was the case with the car dealership example? Sometimes yes, sometimes no. When I get up from the negotiations and leave, I must be prepared to give up the deal. (If I'm not, I should never use this ploy.) But if they do come running after me, I'll know that I can get many more concessions from the sellers.

There are other times when it pays simply to walk away. Maybe you get a chance to think about just how much you are spending or how difficult it's going to be to make the payments. Or maybe after some tough negotiations you think about the home and realize it really isn't the palace you thought it was. You may decide that you really don't want to buy the home!

When that happens, don't get sucked into a deal you don't want simply to be polite. Just take a deep breath, smile confidently at those around you, and say "No!" And stick to it.

77. If I Change My Mind, Can I Withdraw My Offer?

The Quick Answer

You can normally withdraw your offer anytime until the sellers accept it in writing. Even if you give the sellers two days, for example, to accept and only one day has passed and they are still thinking about it, you can withdraw your offer. But once they sign, you're on the hook. (See earlier chapters on the sales agreement and on contingencies.)

The Expanded Answer

The legal complexities of contracts are quite arcane, as any attorney will tell you. And this is a good reason for consulting one when you have a problem with contracts. Having said that however, it must also be said that most agents understand that the general rule has always been that any offer, until accepted, can be withdrawn. The sticky part comes about in determining when the offer has been accepted and when it has been withdrawn.

Generally speaking, the offer has been accepted when the sellers sign (not just orally say they've accepted, but physically sign the agreement) an offer you have made, without any changes to it whatever, *and their acceptance has been conveyed to you*. In other words, theoretically, the sellers could sign. But before they or their agent is able to tell you that they've signed, you could call up and shout out, "I withdraw my offer!"

Is your offer withdrawn or is it too late? Can the sellers hold you to the deal, which you now may not want? Who said what first? This is a quagmire that might take several attorneys and a court to sort out.

In the real world, however, most of the time you won't want to withdraw your offer. (Unless, of course, in the meantime you've found a better house at a fraction of the price.) Also the sellers won't accept so quickly. Usually there's a period of extended negotiations, and you'll have many opportunities to withdraw.

Just remember the following general rules:

- Unless the sellers sign your offer exactly as made without changing anything, you're not on the hook.

- If you make any changes to a counter from the sellers, you are now making a new offer which they can accept or reject.

- You should always put a time limit on any offers or counters you make.

- You can withdraw an offer you make up until the sellers sign their acceptance, without making any changes of any kind, and their acceptance has been conveyed to you.

Knowing these rules is important because otherwise an unscrupulous seller or agent might try to bully you into accepting something that you definitely don't want and aren't required to accept.

9
Should I Get a Home Inspection?

78. Does Every House Need to Be Inspected?

The Quick Answer

Yes, even new ones. There are two good reasons. The first is that no matter how many disclosures the sellers may make, you need to have an independent and competent third party tell you the condition of what you are buying. There may be problems with the property that even the sellers don't know about. Second, if there are problems, you can use them as a negotiating tool to get the sellers to correct them, lower the price because of them, or both.

The Expanded Answer

Home inspections are relatively new. Ten years ago no one even heard of them. Today virtually every buyer (and seller) wants one. And for good reason. Homes have reached the stratosphere in terms of pricing. The medium price for a resale as of this writing is around $125,000 and climbing. It is higher for a new home. In many areas people regularly pay $300,000 or more for a home. At those prices you just can't afford to buy a pig in a poke. You must know what you are getting.

It's also important to understand that there are literally thousands of parts to a home and more than a dozen complete systems. Today's modern home has heating and cooling systems, waste water and potable water systems, electrical, phone, and cable systems to name only a few. In addition, there are the foundation, the chimney, the roof, the floors, the insulation, and dozens of other areas where problems can occur. Unless you happen to be in the building trades and are an expert on these, you won't know if they are in good shape, broken, or ready to fall apart. (Even if you're a plumber, you probably won't know what's right or wrong with the electrical system.)

Further, repairs can be costly. Here is just a sampling of what it can typically cost to repair or replace various items:

Fix roof—$5000 to $10,000 or more

Add insulation—$500 to $2500 or more

Convert galvanized steel plumbing to copper—$5,000 or more

Improve drainage—$500 to $10,000 or more

Fix cracked foundation or slab—$5000 to $50,000 or more

Fix chimney—$2500 to $10,000

Convert 2-wire to 3-wire electrical—$5000 or more

And many, many more

The inspection, hopefully, will reveal most problems. Then you can insist that the sellers fix them, or at least compromise and demand that the sellers pay a substantial portion of the costs.

As noted earlier, you can also use problems the inspection reveals as a lever to force the seller to lower the price. You do this by threatening to back out of the deal unless price concessions are made. (It's important that the sales agreement specify that you have a certain number of days to approve the inspection report and that if you disapprove of items, the deal is off—see Chapter 7). Also, see my book *The Home Inspection Trouble Shooter* (Dearborn, 1995).

79. Should the House Be Inspected Before or After the Sales Agreement Is Signed?

The Quick Answer

As a buyer, you normally can only have the home inspected after the sales agreement is signed and only providing such an inspection is called for in the agreement (something you should insist upon). With increasing frequency, however, sellers today are paying for inspections before they put their homes up for sale so they can find out any potential problems and correct them early on.

The Expanded Answer

Be wary of any inspection report that a seller gives to you. Yes, in many states today sellers are required to provide you with reports of any inspections they may have had. However, accepting a report as a fait accompli has at least three drawbacks:

1. You don't know the quality of the inspector. Perhaps
    there is an inspector in the area who is known for
    having "easy" or lax inspections, and the sellers have
    found this person and used him or her. Maybe such an
    inspector overlooked or simply didn't discover many
    problems.

2. When you are the person ordering the inspection and
    report, not only can you choose the inspector (see the
    next question), but you can also ask the inspector to
    address specific problems you may be concerned
    about. For example, you may feel the house has a cer-
    tain tilt toward one side or the floors are uneven. A
    prepared report may not mention these, but if you
    point them out, an inspector may be able to either
    reassure or caution you regarding them.

3. Finally, as noted below, one of the most important
    parts of the inspection is going along yourself. You
    can't do that if the report is already completed.

I have encountered some buyers who have said something to the effect that "We want to have the home
inspected before we make our offer."

This is akin to putting the cart before the horse. No
sellers in their right minds are going to agree to have an
inspector come tromping through their house, disrupting
their lives, and possibly making a mess if not worse unless
there is a legitimate sale. And no buyer should want to
pay for the inspection unless both buyer and seller have
agreed in writing to price and terms for the sale.

In short, the inspection comes after the sales agreement
has been signed. However, as noted, there is usually
plenty of time for renegotiation as problems crop up.

80. How Do I Find a Good Inspector?

The Quick Answer

Try to get recommendations from real estate agents or other professionals. Look for inspectors who belong to trade organizations such as the American Society of Home Inspectors (ASHI). Make sure the inspector or his or her company has been in business for several years at minimum.

The Expanded Answer

Since having home inspections is such a new field, the inspectors themselves tend to be new at it. Most states have not yet begun licensing home inspectors, although that is sure to come eventually. Currently in many areas all that a person needs to do to become an inspector is print up some business cards and hang out a shingle.

You should consider the background of the inspector. Many are from the building trades, former contractors of one sort or another. However, just because a person knows how to build a new house (or put in plumbing or an electrical system) does not mean they know what to look for when inspecting an existing dwelling.

Your best bet is probably a former city or county building inspector. Often when these people retire, they become private home inspectors, and they usually are good at it. They've seen all sorts of homes as public inspectors, and they usually are up-to-date on the current building code.

Additionally, you may need specific inspections covering such areas as soil, roof, or structure. Your best bet here is someone who has an engineering degree in the field.

Be wary of hiring inspectors who are themselves involved in building or repairs. For example, if the roof inspector you hire happens to be a roofer, his or her opinion is always subject to suspicion. Is this person saying the roof on the property is bad because it really is or because they are looking to get a roofing job? A generally good rule to follow is to hire only those companies for inspections that do not do repair work themselves.

Recently I've noted a number of inspection companies that have found a clever way around this safeguard rule. They claim that they do not do any repair work. This may be a fact; however, they will then recommend another company (in which they may have an interest) that does this type of repair work. This is still a bit like letting the wolf and his brother into the hen house. The best bet is to go for an inspector who, if he or she recommends repair companies, simply hands you a list of names and phone numbers without comment and lets you check them out.

81. Do I Have to Pay for the Inspection?

The Quick Answer

Usually, yes. The theory is that since you're the one who wants inspection and who, presumably, will benefit from it, it's only fair that you should pay for it. Inspections today usually run between $250 and $350.

The Expanded Answer

What seems logical on the surface may not make as much sense when we probe deeper. In a very real sense the home inspection protects the seller as much, if not more, than you the buyer. Here's the reason:

In today's litigious environment, home sellers may be liable for all sorts of defects in their properties. For example, their water heater may be leaking gas. But the sellers may not even be aware of it. If the home should be sold and a fire result from the defective heater, the sellers might be held liable. However, if there's an inspection, it may uncover the problem and the sellers can correct it.

Further, once you've had a home inspection, it is much harder to come back at the sellers to claim that there was a hidden defect in the property. You, after all, had the opportunity to hire any inspector you wanted and to do any kind of inspection work. If the inspection revealed nothing untoward, then how was the poor seller to know there was a problem?

This is not to say, of course, that a home inspection protects the sellers from defects that they knew about and failed to disclose. If, for example, the sellers know that a bathroom toilet has been plugged (as evidenced by the fact that they've had plumbers come in to clear it many times), and they fail to disclose this to the buyers, and if later on, the drain line plugs again, flooding a portion of the house with sewerage, they could be on the hook for repair and cleanup costs.

It's important to remember that an inspection is different from a disclosure. An inspection's purpose is to uncover possible problems with the house. The disclosure's purpose is to let the sellers tell you of problems of which they are aware. You need both, and often you want the home inspector to verify or amplify on items that the sellers disclose. There is no charge for the disclosure and today most states require it of sellers.

82. Should I Go Along When the House Is Inspected?

The Quick Answer

Absolutely yes. If at all possible, arrange for the inspection to occur at a time when you can get off work. If necessary, it can be done in the evening or on a weekend. You will get more for your money and invariably learn a great deal more if you accompany the home inspector.

The Expanded Answer

There are, in reality, two types of inspection reports. The formal written reports that the home inspector hands to you after the inspection are one type of a report. The informal comments that the inspector makes while conducting the inspection could be considered another type of a report. The big difference is that the inspector will be held to anything put down on paper; hence most written reports contain as many disclaimers as they do hard facts, and most of those facts tend to be equivocated. On the other hand, most inspectors are quite candid during the actual inspection. They will chat with you and give you their opinion on this or that. In short, you tend to learn far more during the inspector's informal comments than from the written report.

Further, if you accompany the inspector, you can direct him or her to areas of concern to you. For example, there may be a retaining wall in the side yard that's holding back a hillside. Is that retaining wall in good shape? Is the drainage correct? Does it need work or replacement? You can ask these questions on the spot and, presuming your inspector is good at the job, get direct answers such as, "It looks like it will last another 10 years." On a written report, however, you might end up with a statement such as, "Retaining wall on south side of property is not new and could require maintenance or replacement at some point in the future." Not very helpful at all, but it does protect the inspector's backside.

Going along also lets you get an opinion of the inspector. Does she or he wear appropriate clothes, have all necessary tools, and go about the job in a businesslike fashion? Or does the person have to keep going back to the truck for this tool or that, seem to forget to check items that you remind him or her of, and in general seem lost at what he or she is doing? Does the inspector actually crawl into the attic to check on the insulation? Does the inspector crawl around under the house and in the basement to check on bracing, on ground water accumulating, and on damage to the foundation? Going along lets you be sure that the inspector is doing all that he or she is being paid for.

Finally, there's the matter that an inspection is not always the cleanest job. You might have to crawl in dirty, muddy places or climb onto rafters. All of which is to say, wear old clothes that can be discarded, and don't worry if your hands get a little dirty. If you want to go where a good home inspector goes, you can't wear a business suit or be squeamish about a little dirt.

83. Should the Inspector Check for Hazardous Materials?

The Quick Answer

If possible, yes. The trouble is that inspecting for such items as lead paint, radon gas, asbestos, and so on can be a difficult and time-consuming job, often requiring specialized equipment and testing. A general home inspection will probably not go into detail on these items, although it may alert you to the possibility that these exist. You can hire a specialist to check them out.

The Expanded Answer

Today as never before, we are all conscious of the environmental hazards that could be in the home. In the past we never cared about lead paint that (prior to 1978 when it was banned) was frequently used for trim and in bathrooms and kitchens, for example. We did not know about the dangers of asbestos, which used to be commonly used to line furnaces and ducts. Today, however, we are increasingly aware of these and other toxic materials and the dangers they could pose. The real question, however, is how concerned are we?

As of 1997, by federal law all sellers of single-family as well as many multiple-family homes must provide buyers with a statement about the lead paint in the home and with a booklet which describes the dangers as well as give you 10 days to check it out. However, as of this writing this is a regulation without teeth. All the sellers have to do is to say that they are unaware of any lead paint in the home (which is probably true), and this statement satisfies their disclosure requirements. (Lead paint was banned in 1978.) If you want to pursue the issue further, you must hire a lead paint inspector at a cost usually exceeding $300.

There are no federal regulations with regard to many other toxic materials which could be in the home, such as asbestos or radon. Again, if you are concerned about these, you will need to hire a specialist to check them out.

In some areas there are additional concerns that go beyond toxic into natural catastrophes. For example, has the home been retrofitted to withstand an earthquake. (This is a big issue in areas such as California and other earthquake prone regions.) Similarly, is the house protected against hurricanes, tornadoes, or whatever else mother nature may throw against it in the particular region in which it is located? An overall home inspection may reveal some of this, but you may want to hire a specialist to check out the home for you.

It usually comes down to concern and money. You can literally spend thousands of dollars on home inspections. If they reveal nothing, your pocketbook will be thinner, but your mind should be more at ease. On the other hand, if something is found, such as lead paint on the outside trim of the house, what are you going to do about it? Lead paint removal (like asbestos removal) requires experts, is itself dangerous, and if not done properly, could contaminate larger areas. In short, it's very expensive. Most home owners, who have lived with it, are simply unwilling to pay upwards of $10,000 for lead paint removal so the next occupant can feel safe from the threat. Of course, you could always pay the price…or you could not purchase the home and look elsewhere. That, ultimately, is the choice you get by having the home inspected for hazardous materials.

84. Can I Use the Inspection Report to Get a Lower Price?

The Quick Answer

Sometimes. If the inspection report comes up with a serious problem, you can often get the sellers to reduce their price to compensate for it. Keep in mind, however, that the sellers could always elect to fix the problem themselves and often will do this if they determine that the fix is cheaper than the price reduction you may be demanding.

The Expanded Answer

The inspection report has become a negotiating tool that has been wielded with surprising effectiveness by some buyers. The trick seems to be to convince the sellers of the gravity of the problem that has been revealed but at the same time figure a way to actually accomplish the fix for a bargain price.

For example, I had described this technique in an earlier book and a couple wrote to tell me their story. They found a house that they very much wanted. However, the foundation had sunk somewhat in the back so that the back side of the house was lower than the front. If you had a rubber ball and laid it down at the front of the house, it would roll to the back on the wood floors.

A contractor had been summoned for an evaluation and had determined that the house would have to be lifted off the existing foundation and moved. Then that foundation would have be removed using jack hammers. Finally, a new foundation would have to be poured, and the house brought back and lowered onto it. The total cost was estimated to be a minimum of $50,000!

Needless to say, the sellers were distraught. However, the buyers said that since they really wanted the home, they were willing to contribute toward the fixing of the place. The wanted the sellers to reduce their price by $35,000. After some soul searching, the sellers agreed.

After the buyers took possession, they had the home lifted on jacks (but not moved) and shims inserted between the existing foundation and the structure. The house was thus leveled. The cost was $3500. In addition, they spent another $2500 on drainage to be sure that the foundation in the rear did not sink any further.

These buyers used the leverage of the inspection report to get a dramatic price reduction, then used creative thinking to solve a serious problem. Can you do the same? Sometimes. It's important to remember that some problems just cost a lot of money to fix. And others cannot be postponed. (You might get the sellers to reduce the price because the house has a bad roof, but if you don't spend the bucks to get it fixed, it will leak on you!)

85. What If the Inspection Reveals a Very Serious Problem?

The Quick Answer

Sometimes the best thing you can do is to walk away. Not all problems have solutions, at least not those we would like to hear about. Sometimes the problem is just too severe. To buy the home, no matter what concessions the sellers make, might be to assume an unsurmountable problem.

The Expanded Answer

The real question is how do you determine when the problem is too severe to tackle? The answer is that you will undoubtedly know it when you see it.

The worst problems I have seen have dealt with foundations. In one case, a natural stream flowed right under a house. It was dry during the summer months, but during the winter rainy season there could be quite a strong flow of water. Over the years, the stream had undermined and broken up the foundation until now the home was barely standing on a couple of supports.

Because the property was in a very desirable neighborhood, the sellers had no end of potential buyers. However, those who were wise simply passed. To fix the problem might have involved locating the source of the stream and changing its course, something that probably would have been impossible in a residential neighborhood. The truth of the matter was that the house should never have been built where it was. The lot should have been left vacant. The home actually had no real value, and any buyers who purchased it would have been throwing away their money.

Of course, not all situations are so obvious. In another case, the home was built on a cut-and-fill lot. It was on a hillside and the developer had cut a notch out of the hill and then used the dirt removed to fill below the lot. As a result the portion of the house on the cut section was solid, but the fill section was sinking and the house on that portion was tipping down.

It might have been possible to temporarily shore up the foundation on the drooping side and level the house. But until the land beneath could be stabilized so that it would no longer sink, no permanent solution would be found. And stabilizing moving earth is a difficult proposition.

Finally, in yet another situation an inspection revealed a buried diesel oil tank that seemed to be leaking. When I saw this property, I ran, not walked away even though the sellers, understandably, were anxious to negotiate. Any item which can be labeled toxic (as can diesel fuel) and which is in the ground can be costly almost beyond belief to remove. It can require special crews, who may have to haul dirt hundreds of miles away to a toxic dump site. Cleanup can cost in the hundreds of thousands of dollars. Further, as soon as your name goes on the title, even if you own the property for only a few months, you might be held liable for the entire cleanup. (It's easy to see why I beat such a hasty retreat!)

Of course, not all situations are this bad. However, some are and others are even worse. Be wary of very serious problems. Usually it's better to let the sellers worry about them.

86. What If the Sellers Fail to Disclose Serious Problems?

The Quick Answer

Disclosures are required by sellers in most states. However, few states have strict disclosure laws. (California is an exception—it has amongst the strictest.) If sellers fail to disclose a serious problem, particularly one of which they were aware, you, the agent, and the sellers may work out a money settlement to you. You also may have the right to go to court to claim payment for damages you may have sustained as a result. In addition, in some situations you can ask for rescission, the return of the home to the sellers and your money to you.

The Expanded Answer

As a practical matter, suing over the sellers' failure to disclose can be expensive, time-consuming, and the results can be mixed. However, sometimes it may be necessary.

In one situation, sellers did not disclose that their pets had urinated on the carpeting throughout the home they were selling. When the buyers saw the home, the windows were always open and the sellers kept a batch of herbs and spice brewing on the stove to give the place a homey aroma.

However, the first night the buyers moved in proved horrendous to them. It was cold so they closed all the windows and turned on the heat. The odors wafting up from the carpeting were so strong they made their eyes water. Soon the children were coughing. The smell literally drove the buyers out of the home and into a motel, where they stayed.

Of course, the buyers immediately informed the sellers, who said they were shocked and were willing to pay for new carpeting. The buyers had the old carpeting and padding ripped out and then much of the flooring, because it had likewise been stained and the odor could not be removed. The final cost was $17,000.

The sellers balked at this, so the buyers took them to court. (It did not hurt that one of the buyers was herself an attorney.) They ultimately won and got their money.

In other cases, however, sellers have stonewalled buyers, claimed they were unaware of the problem or said it was not as severe as the buyers alleged, and they prevailed. As a result, often buyers will make as much of an argument as they can, but often will back down before going all the way to court. A lot depends, of course, on how badly damaged they have been.

In most cases, the matter is resolved through some form of negotiation or arbitration. The sellers come up with some money, usually less than the buyers are asking, and the buyers agree to drop the matter. On the other hand, in states with strict disclosure laws, the state itself may help the buyers pursue their claim.

87. Do I Need a Separate Termite Inspection Report?

The Quick Answer

You certainly do, if you plan on getting almost any kind of financing. In virtually all areas of the country, lenders require a termite clearance before funding a loan. No clearance, no mortgage. You may also want one for personal reasons, just to be sure your house doesn't have bugs!

The Expanded Answer

The report normally covers termite infestation as well as dry rot and some other conditions. The inspector checks out all accessible areas of the home and either issues an all clear, certifying the home free from pests (the clearance is usually good for about 120 days), or indicates areas where pests were found and that the problem must be corrected before a clearance is issued.

   If problems are found, they are usually in one of three categories. Category 1 is mandatory repairs. Termites, dry rot, or some other pest condition was found, and the pest must be removed and damaged materials often must be replaced. When you see a house with a tent over it, this is usually category 1 work. The seller normally pays for this.

   Category 2 work usually is preventive in nature. No pests were found, a window should be recaulked to keep moisture out or debris moved away from the house to prevent future termite infestation. This is optional work which the buyers usually pay for. If you don't want to do it, you don't have to.

Finally, the last category reflects problems that aren't covered by 1 or 2. For example, the inspector found moisture under the house. It's not category 1, because there were no pests. It's not category 2, because it's unlikely to cause a future pest problem. It's just noted for the attention of buyers and sellers. Usually corrective work here is not done. If it is, it's up to negotiation as to who pays for it.

It's important to understand that either party can pay for any or all of the work. It depends on what was agreed upon in the sales contract. As a buyer, however, don't agree to pay for repairs (category 1 work) unless you have a very good reason for doing so (such as you're "stealing" the place for an incredibly low price).

In most areas, lenders are only concerned about the house itself, not unattached decks, awnings, sheds, and so on. If that's the case, sometimes a clearance can be obtained, even if pests are noted in those unattached areas, without having to do category 1 work. This can sometimes work to your benefit. For example, I once bought a home that had severe dry rot damage to an unattached deck. The cost of deck replacement was $3500. However, the following agreement was reached: it was pointed out to the termite company that the deck was not attached, and over some objections, a clearance was obtained. Then, the sellers gave me a $2500 allowance in the form of nonrecurring closing costs, because of the deck problem I was assuming. This saved the seller $1000 in deck repair and helped make the deal. I later put in a new deck myself at a cost of about $700 in materials, saving me some money as well.

A note of caution: beware of termite inspectors who insist on checking out the shower pan, particularly on second floor or higher levels. This involves plugging the shower drain and filling the bottom of the shower with water. If the pan leaks, water can pour down through ceilings and onto walls and floors doing considerable damage. Since you, as the buyer, required the inspection, some sellers will try to blame you for the damage and may ask you to pay for it. (Some states, such as California, may prohibit checking shower pans.)

In most areas the seller pays for the cost of having a termite inspection.

10

How Do I Cut My Closing Costs?

88. How Will I Know What My Closing Costs Will Be?

The Quick Answer

The Real Estate Settlement Procedures Act (RESPA) requires that your mortgage lender give you a statement which will break down all of your costs. It won't protect you against unwarranted charges—it just lets you know what are all of the charges against you at closing.

The Expanded Answer

The real question for most buyers is not so much what will the charges be (like death and taxes, most can't be avoided), but when will you find out about them and what can you do about unwarranted ones? If you learn of unwarranted charges on the day you are set to close, it's a bit late to do anything. That's why your lender will give you a good-faith estimate of your closing costs at the time you apply for a mortgage. These may not be complete in that they may not cover all prorations and some other charges, but they should tell you what your charge for obtaining a mortgage will be as well as give you an estimate of escrow and title insurance fees, if any.

If you are dealing with a good real estate agent, that agent will prepare a list of your estimated charges even before you make your offer! The idea here is to show you what your true costs are so you can better decide how much to offer on the property. One agent I knew used to claim that she could come within $20 of the actual charges and most of the time, she did!

Keep in mind that there could be some sizable expenses to pay for the closing including the following:

- *Points on your loan.*   You should be told the number of points by the lender, up front. Remember, each point is worth 1 percent of the loan amount. If you must pay 2.5 points on a $200,000 mortgage, that's $5000.

- *Escrow and title insurance fees.*   These are usually based on the sales price. The higher the sales price, the higher the charges will be for these fees. Keep in mind that escrow and title companies compete and that one may therefore be slightly less or more than another.

- *Attorney's fee.*   Usually the attorney's fee is around $1000 or less in states where attorney's are regularly used.

- *Agent's commission.*   This commission is paid by you only if you used a buyer's agent and agreed to pay the commission instead of its being paid by the seller.

- *Prorations.*   Taxes, insurance, rent, or other prorations could be next to nothing or amount to thousands of dollars.

- *Other fees.*   These are usually in connection with the mortgage (see questions 90 and 91).

Determining just what your closing costs will be shouldn't be a difficult or arcane procedure. If your agent can't or won't do it, have the escrow officer or your attorney do it. Anyone familiar with real estate transactions should be able to come up with a very close estimate in short order.

89. Can I Get the Seller to Pay My Closing Costs?

The Quick Answer

Maybe. Who pays some closing costs, such as escrow and title insurance fees, is usually determined by local custom. On the other hand, all mortgage fees are normally paid for by the buyers. However, everything in real estate is negotiable. If you work out a deal where the sellers agree to pay your closing costs, so be it. Just keep in mind, however, that you can have some problems with lenders and even possibly even with the IRS if the sellers agree to pay your recurring mortgage costs.

The Expanded Answer

As noted, who pays what is determined largely by local custom. For example, in northern California the buyers normally pay both escrow and title insurance charges, two of the biggest closing fees. In southern California it's the opposite with sellers normally toting the bill. (If you sell in the north and move to the south to buy, you'll make out like a bandit; go the other way and it costs you a fortune!)

At the time you make your purchase, however, you can write into the purchase contract any arrangement that you and the sellers agree upon. For example, you may make it a deal point that the sellers pay all of your nonrecurring closing costs. You won't buy unless they agree.

They're anxious to sell and are otherwise satisfied with the deal, so they accept. The sellers now pay for the escrow, title insurance, attorney fees, and so on—everything that occurs only once at the close of the deal.

Beware of insisting the sellers pay for your recurring closing costs. This includes prorated interest on your mortgage, some fees, and some points calculated into your mortgage annual percentage rate (APR). If the sellers pay for these, the lenders may take this to mean you're getting help with the sale and loan, and it could affect your ability to qualify for the mortgage. Also, as a property owner, you normally take a deduction for interest and taxes from your personal income taxes. However, if the sellers paid some of your interest and taxes in the year you bought, the Internal Revenue Service might take a dim view of your claiming the full deduction. Check with your accountant here.

90. Can I Get the Lender to Cut Its Closing Costs?

The Quick Answer

Yes, no, and maybe. An individual lender may simply be set up to charge a set number of fees, and like a computer program, these come spitting out with no room for variation. On the other hand, you can select your lender, and there is sometimes an enormous difference in charges. So, while you may not be able to get an individual lender to reduce fees, you may be able to pay far less by shopping for a less expensive lender.

The Expanded Answer

The time to shop for a lender is when you are first applying for a mortgage. It is at that point that you have the greatest leverage. If the lender charges too much, you can walk out and look elsewhere. (There's no shortage of mortgage lenders.)

On the other hand, if you wait until you're ready to close to determine that the charges are too high, you're probably out of luck. Changing lenders takes time—for a new appraisal and for a new round of qualifying. It's like starting all over again. Many sellers simply won't tolerate the wait, but will insist you close with the lender you've got or lose the deal and potentially your deposit, too. Further, it's also costly. If nothing else, you'll probably have to pay for a new credit report and appraisal. (It seems that each lender uses a different appraiser and for some reason simply can't bear to use an appraisal that you might have already paid for. The credit report only costs around $35, so it usually isn't a big deal.)

What you need to do is to very carefully read the estimate of costs that the lender gives to you. Know how many points you will have to pay as well as what all of the other fees may be. If you don't agree with a fee, speak up and tell the lender. In some cases, particularly when the market is cold and there aren't many new financings coming along, a lender may reduce or even eliminate a charge. On the other hand, if the market is hot and there are people waiting in line to get financing, don't expect the lender to budge.

Note: we're talking primarily about charges in addition to the interest rate and the points on the mortgage. These are usually (but not always) competitive. You can shop around for these simply by calling up different lenders or mortgage brokers and asking what are the best points and rate you can get. Also, rate and points are often posted in big, bold letters on the documents you will be asked to sign. It's the other charges that are located in the fine print that you usually want to watch out for.

91. How Can I Avoid Paying "Garbage" Closing Costs?

The Quick Answer

"Garbage" closing costs are extra and unwarranted fees tacked on to your mortgage costs. They can often add up to several hundred dollars or more. You can avoid paying them by protesting to your lender. However, if the lender refuses to remove them, your only choice may be to seek a different lender.

The Expanded Answer

The key here is to take action early on. The reason is that the lender can add in all sorts of fees, as long as they are clearly disclosed to you. If you protest the fees, some lenders will remove them. But if they don't, and if you've waited until your mortgage has been granted and escrow is ready to close, it's probably too late to do anything.

Garbage fees are sometimes tacked on by the originator of the loan and not the lender. For example, the mortgage broker, a person or company that acts as an intermediary for a lender, retailing loans so to speak, might add fees that are in addition to the fees that the lender imposes. These fees, which go directly into the mortgage broker's pocket, may not be justified. (Keep in mind that the mortgage broker is receiving a fee directly from the lender for placing the loan.)

Some typical garbage fees might include the following:

Loan document preparation.   Anything more than $25 is probably garbage. These days it only takes a few taps of a computer's keys to spit out a mortgage document.

Lender's attorney's fee.   The lender should have attorneys on staff to handle the legal aspects of a mortgage, and that should be the lender's expense, not yours.

Loan origination fee. The job of the retailer is to originate loans; that's what the lender is paying him for. You shouldn't have to pay for it, too. (Note: this is different from the "origination fee" points sometimes charged in FHA loans. Also adding to the confusion, some lenders call their points origination fees.)

Secretarial fees. Unless this was for your own secretary, it's garbage.

Packaging fee. This is an originator's charge for packaging your mortgage for presentation to a lender or from the lender for putting your mortgage together with others for sale to a secondary lender. Either way it's a normal cost of doing business, and you shouldn't have to pay it.

Underwriting fee. Many loans must be underwritten and this costs the lender something, often under $100. Again, it's a normal cost of doing business and shouldn't be passed on to you.

92. Should I Take My Attorney to the Closing?

The Quick Answer

It's a good idea. Many buyers who are experienced in real estate transactions feel perfectly comfortable going to the closing themselves. However, if this is your first home purchase or you are unfamiliar with the closing procedure, then you would be well advised to have an attorney with you to explain what's going on and to check for errors.

The Expanded Answer

The *closing* is where you sign the mortgage documents, agree to give the seller the money for the purchase, and execute other documents needed to finalize the transaction. Typically, it is handled in an escrow or title insurance office. On the East Coast it may be handled in an attorney's office.

Don't expect all of the closing documents to be prepared correctly. Often there are mistakes, particularly in the math. Sometimes even the loan documents contain errors. For example, the interest rate may be wrong or the conditions of an adjustable rate mortgage may be different than what you agreed to. (Usually it's just a matter of the lender sending in the wrong documents.) You want to be able to detect the errors and get them corrected on the spot. To sign now and hope for the best later on is not an advisable course of action.

Many buyers mistakenly believe that their real estate agent wil! accompany them to the closing to explain things. After all, the agent was helpful in finding the house and in conducting the negotiations. It's only natural to expect the agent to continue being helpful right through the close of the deal.

Most agents, however, will not accompany you to the closing and will not advise you on what you are signing and whether or not the document is correctly prepared. The reason is liability—they don't want to be liable for any errors or mistakes that occur at closing. In addition, you may need and ask for legal advice; because very few agents are also attorneys, they cannot provide you with such information.

Also, don't expect the title or escrow company officer to provide you with much in the way of explanations or advice. They may say something such as, "This is the mortgage note," or "This is the proration schedule." But if you ask them to elaborate, they may simply add, "It's what the lender sent…"

You are on your own at the closing. As noted, many experienced buyers feel perfectly comfortable with this. If you don't, then your attorney is the one to provide you with advice.

93. Do I Really Need a Title Search and Title Insurance?

The Quick Answer

Yes, absolutely. These are two of the most important parts of buying real estate. You never want to be without either, even if it means that you must pay the charges.

The Expanded Answer

A title search is done by the title insurance company. It looks backward along the chain of ownership of the property you are buying. It can reveal vital pieces of information. For example, it confirms (or denies) that the seller is, in fact, the true owner of the property. It also exposes any liens or judgments against the seller, or anyone else, that may have been placed on the property. In short, it tells you the condition of the title to the property you are buying. The title insurance guarantees that you're getting good, clear title.

Title insurance, however, won't be issued until any "clouds" or items affecting the title have been cleared up. For example, the sellers may have failed to pay off a loan at some time in the past, and the lender secured a judgment against them and then recorded that judgment as a lien against the title. The sellers must now remove the lien in order to give you clear title.

Or perhaps there's some confusion about the names of the sellers. The title is recorded in a slightly different version of the sellers' names. This too must be cleared up.

Almost anything can cloud a title. The sellers may have contracted for some work done to the house, and there was a dispute with the contractor, who filed a mechanic's lien. The government can file a lien for unpaid taxes. There might even be a lien incorrectly filed against a former owner of the property. All of these must be cleared up before you can get good title to the property.

It is normally the job of the sellers to clear the title. However, some gentle encouragement occasionally given by the buyers can sometimes help.

Beyond the standard form of title insurance issued by title companies, they can also issue a more comprehensive form called an ALTA (American Land Title Association). Here the title insurance company actually sends someone out to the property to confirm that the house is properly on the land and that it's not situated on someone else's property and that there are no other apparent physical defects. Generally, an ALTA is required by most lenders. It protects them, not you. But, you must pay for it, if you want the loan.

94. What Should I Bring to the Closing?

The Quick Answer

The only thing you really need is your checkbook! I suggest that you also bring along your copy of the sales agreement, the estimate of loan costs your lender originally gave you, and a small pocket calculator.

The Expanded Answer

Actually, you will need a cashier's check for most of the money. The escrow officer or attorney handling the closing will be able to tell you the amount (for the down payment plus most closing costs) needed some days before closing. You then should have ample time to get to your bank to get the cashier's check.

Because of the fact that in some special cases payment can be stopped even on a cashier's check, it often takes a few days after all documents have been signed and you have paid the money before escrow closes. This allows the escrow officer or the attorney to be sure the check has been accepted and paid by your bank.

You will also need your regular checkbook. This is to pay for a number of other small items that will not be covered by the cashier's check. This should amount to less than a thousand dollars, but sometimes could be more—check with the closer to see how much you should have available in your checking account.

I also recommend that you bring a copy of the sales agreement. (It should be available in the packet of closing documents, but not necessarily.) If you have a question about anything in the closing statement, you can refer back to the sales agreement, which is normally the ruling document.

Also, your lender will have given you a fair estimate of loan and closing costs when you first applied for your mortgage. Bring this along to compare with the actual costs. Anything substantially higher or anything added should be challenged.

Finally, a small pocket calculator can be invaluable. Escrow officers and attorneys who close deals are notorious for making errors in addition and subtraction. Check all the figures. Don't rely on an error being caught and corrected later on. Maybe it will. Maybe it won't. You do the math, and you'll feel a lot better.

11

What Should I Do to Prepare to Move In?

95. What If the Seller Wants to Stay an Extra Day or Two in the House After Closing?

The Quick Answer

It's a bad idea. The last thing you want is to gain ownership (have title switched to your name and begin paying on the mortgage) and not be able to gain possession. The real problem is not the day or two extra the sellers may want. It's what do you do if you say okay, and then the sellers, for whatever reason, don't move out!

The Expanded Answer

There are many reasons that sellers may have for wanting to stay a few extra days. Their arrangements for moving may not have been well coordinated, and the movers will be there on Monday instead of the anticipated previous Friday.

Or, their plans may have gone awry, and they have no place to immediately move to—they want to stay a couple of extra weeks.

Or, someone in the family gets sick, and it's inconvenient to move when previously planned.

Or...the list of reasons can be an arm's-length long.

While each case has to be judged on its own merits, the general rule is that you always want to get possession of the property at the close of escrow. That makes for a clean deal and a good transition. I always insist that the sellers be out of the property by the date of closing, before I sign the closing papers. (I have bought where the sellers were in the process of moving at the time of closing and not yet completely out—but their intentions were quite clear.)

If for any reason the sellers remain in possession of the property after the close of escrow, then they usually have the rights of tenants. If for some reason you decide to let them stay, be sure you have them execute a strong tenancy agreement that provides for a substantial security and cleaning deposit and for their paying for attorney's fees in the event they have to be evicted. They should also pay rent at least equal to your costs, including mortgage payment, taxes, insurance, and any utilities you're carrying.

In a worst-case situation, the sellers remain in possession of the property and refuse to move. Your course of action then probably would be an unlawful detainer lawsuit, in other words, an eviction. In most areas this takes about a month and around a thousand dollars, if it is not contested. If the sellers feel they have reason to contest the eviction, it could take much longer and cost much more.

All of which is to say that things can get sticky pretty fast if you let the sellers retain possession after the deal closes. While every situation is different and you may, indeed, feel that you want to give the sellers a few extra days to move out, in general its best to insist on possession at the close of escrow. This is one situation were being a "nice guy" can bring you lots of headaches.

96. Where and When Do I Get the Key?

The Quick Answer

This should be easy, but sometimes it's not. Turning over the key amounts to giving you possession of the property. Often the real estate agent can handle this although some times you'll need to deal directly with the sellers. Be sure you set up a specific date, time, and place for the transfer.

The Expanded Answer

Be sure you make specific arrangements for receiving the key. Sometimes you'll be told, "We'll leave it under the door mat." This could work out fine, or not. What if there were some damage to the property? The sellers could say it was vandalism; kids found the key under the door mat (which you agreed to), got in and did the damage. It's not their fault. They want you to turn the matter over to your insurance company. Now you've got a headache.

An active transfer of possession by physically receiving the key is probably best. You meet the sellers or their agent at the property, quickly look around to make sure it's in good shape (not an inspection, just a quick look around), and get the key. It's neat and clean this way.

Once you get the key, be sure you take the locks off all the outside doors and get them to a locksmith to have the keys changed. This is not to imply that the sellers would later come back and break into the property. It's just that you have no way of knowing who had access to the old keys. It could have been workpeople in the area, friends and relatives of the sellers, anyone at all. By having the locks changed you protect yourself.

97. How Soon Should I Connect the Utilities, Phone, Cable, etc.?

The Quick Answer

This is of particular concern if you are a first-time home buyer. You want to contact the utility and other companies as early as possible to make arrangements. It's important to give them a specific day, usually the anticipated close of escrow, to have everything turned on in your name.

The Expanded Answer

The theory here is that when working with utility companies, it is far easier to have them change the date, than to get them to commit to turning on the service. If you haven't previously had service with the company (you may be from out of the area or may have been renting before and the landlord may have paid for some or all of your utilities), you will probably have to fill out a credit application. You may also be required to put down a deposit. (Usually the deposit is returned after you've paid your utility bill on time for six months or so.)

In short, it could take several weeks or longer for the utilities, phone, cable, and so on to get you authorized and to give you a connect date. However, my own experience is that once all of the formalities are completed, it's only a matter of a quick phone call to have that date changed. If it turns out escrow is going to close a week earlier or later, it's now a simple matter of calling the utility to have them move up or delay the hookups. The rule here is to plan as far ahead as possible. You don't want to move and have no electricity, water, or phone.

98. What If After I Move In I Discover New Damage to the Home or Something Missing?

The Quick Answer

The house should be virtually the same as it was for your final walk through. (You did have a final walk-through inspection, didn't you? See question 66.) If something was taken that shouldn't have been (such as window coverings) or if there was damage, don't panic. Contact the agent and/or the seller immediately. In most cases a solution can be quickly and amicably worked out.

The Expanded Answer

It's important to understand that if there was still furniture in the house when you last saw it, moving it out may reveal scratches and scuff marks on the walls or floors. This is normal and to be expected. Unless you're buying a brand-new and previously unlived in house, the place will show some wear and tear. That's why most buyers figure on spending a few days cleaning and painting before they move in.

Anything more serious is a different matter. If the sellers took something they weren't supposed to, a simple phone call can usually rectify the situation. In the vast majority of cases, they simply didn't understand that the throw rug or the dining room chandelier belongs to you and will return the item, usually quite shamefaced.

If there was real damage, such as a hole in the wall or a broken window, the sellers may or may not even be aware of it. The movers may have done it without telling them.

Once again, a quick phone call is usually all that's necessary.

On the other hand, if the sellers refuse to return the item or correct the problem, you must decide how big an issue to make of it. I use the $100 rule of thumb. If the problem (or total of all problems) is worth under $100, it's probably not worth much time and effort (not to mention the high blood pressure!) in correcting it. If it's over $100, maybe it is. See question 100 for when to call your attorney.

99. What If the Appliances, Heater, or Air Conditioner Don't Work?

The Quick Answer

Unless you bought the home with the written understanding that it, or the appliances were sold "as is," it's implied that they will work. The seller normally warrants this to the home warranty insurance company (assuming one was used on the deal). A call will usually get someone out fairly quickly to fix the item, although you may have to pay a deductible. If there's no home warranty plan on the house, the seller usually will pay for it. (You could, ultimately, have to take a reluctant seller to small-claims court to get satisfaction here, which is another reason to insist on a home warranty insurance plan.)

The Expanded Answer

This is a great reason for having the sellers buy you a home protection plan. The plans normally cover all built-in appliances, and for an additional fee will cover such items as the air-conditioning and even a spa.

However, if the problem occurs when you first move in, in other words, the stove doesn't work right from the beginning, the home protection company may balk at paying for it, stating (with some justification) that it was obviously broken when the sellers had it and, consequently, doesn't come under the plan. (The plans normally cover items that are in good working condition at the time of the transfer of title.)

If this is the case, then you will need to call the agent and/or the sellers. You may get into a situation of each party denying responsibility—the sellers saying it worked fine when they left, the protection company saying it didn't.

Usually these things get worked out. The most common solution is for the protection company to pay for the problem, less the deductible. After all, if the sellers say it was working fine when they left, who's to prove it wasn't?

Additionally, in a situation like this where the problem arises immediately, the sellers will usually cough up the money for the deductible. In other words, it usually only costs you a couple of phone calls, but no money out of pocket.

If there is no home protection plan in place, then you'll need to demand that the sellers fix it. In most cases, they will. If not, then see question 100.

100. When Is a Problem Big Enough to Call My Attorney?

The Quick Answer

If you don't get satisfaction—if the damage is not fixed, the item not returned, or the appliance not repaired, my suggestion is that you first lean on the agent. He or she will in turn lean on the sellers, explaining that you are within your rights to have all the property you are entitled to in working condition. If that doesn't work, consider small claims court. Only if the problem is a big one, in my opinion, should you get an attorney involved.

The Expanded Answer

The difficulty with going to an attorney is that it can become costly very quickly. Moreover, you never know for sure if you will prevail.

Often it's far better to be the squeaky wheel that gets the oil, than to become the plaintiff in a lawsuit. Get assertive with the real estate agent. He or she should be on the ball and see that this sort of thing doesn't happen. (I have sometimes seen real estate agents themselves pay for the repair or replacement of small items just to avoid getting into a shouting match between buyers and sellers, though I wouldn't count on it every time.)

If agent and sellers won't budge, then I suggest that you use the $100 rule noted in question 98. If it's under $100, I just forget it. It's not worth the hassle.

If it's over $100, particularly far over, then I reevaluate. It can cost $50 to have an attorney send a first letter. However, very often just receiving a letter from an attorney will spur people to action. If they see that you've gone that far, they may believe you're determined enough to carry this onward, and they may capitulate—your problem's solved.

On the other hand, if the sellers adamantly refuse to fix the problem, then it's a matter of how much money and time you want to spend to get satisfaction. All areas of the country have a small-claims court, although the maximum amount you can sue for varies. There are many excellent books on the market telling you how to proceed here, and you can pursue the claim yourself.

On the other hand, a full-blown lawsuit conducted by an attorney may cost $5000 at minimum and could run much more.

Going to court should be considered only as a last resort. As noted, in most cases a couple of phone calls will solve the problem or at most an attorney's letter. However, when the issue is big enough, then by all means consider small-claims court and as a last resort, a lawsuit.

(If you sue, try to sue for the attorney's fees and court costs as well.)

101. What If I Decide I Really Don't Want the House, After I've Moved In?

The Quick Answer

It's called *buyer's remorse* and usually hits your first night in the home. You begin thinking about those huge mortgage payments, the taxes, the utilities, the garden, and say to yourself, "What have I gotten myself into?!" Be calm, it normally passes in a day or two.

The Expanded Answer

Buyer's remorse often occurs whenever we've made a much larger than normal purchase. A house very definitely qualifies here. It's normal. It's understandable. It will pass.

On the other hand, if you're truly unhappy with the purchase, give it some time. Keep in mind, however, that unless there is some very serious defect that the sellers failed to disclose, the property is definitely yours. (If there is a very serious defect, you could sue for rescission—force the sellers to repay you your money and take the property back—but you'd better have darn good reasons before proceeding, be prepared for what could be a long, bitter, and very expensive fight, and be prepared for mixed results.)

My suggestion is that you give yourself some time. If eventually you find that for whatever reason you feel you can't stand the place, consider your other alternatives: You can move to some place else and rent the house you just bought. This may be a good alternative when you can't quickly resell and recoup your investment. You can resell, but keep in mind that an quick resale will undoubtedly be costly. You'll have to pay a commission (unless you sell it yourself) plus closing costs all over again. Or you can live there and grin and bear it.

Buying a home is not a matter to be taken lightly. Be sure it's what you really want before you make the commitment.

Index

Index

About the Author

Robert Irwin has been a successful real estate broker for more than 30 years, helping buyers and sellers alike through every kind of real estate transaction. He also serves as a consultant to lenders, investors, and brokers. Irwin is one of the most knowledgeable and prolific writers in the real estate field, with such books to his credit as *Tips & Traps When Selling a Home*; *Tips & Traps When Buying a Home*; *Tips & Traps When Mortgage Hunting*; *Tips & Traps for Making Money in Real Estate*; *Tips & Traps for Saving on All Your Real Estate Taxes*; *Buy, Rent & Hold*; *How to Find Hidden Real Estate Bargains*; and *The McGraw-Hill Real Estate Handbook*. Robert Irwin is based in Los Angeles, California.